MORE THAN A WALK ON THE BEACH

CONFESSIONS OF AN UNLIKELY DIPLOMAT

by Ambassador Mary E. Kramer {Ret.}

Kevin

Enjoy the book.

All the best

Mary Kramer

Ambassador Mary E. Kramer {Ret.}

13598 Village Court

Clive, Iowa 50325

© 2010

Library of Congress Control Number: 2010936764

ISBN Number: ISBN-13 978-1-888223-93-4

THANKS

To President George W. Bush for giving me the opportunity to serve my country as an ambassador.

To the team at Sigler Companies who gave advice early on in the process and then made the project a reality at the end.

To the team at the Foster Group - I could not have completed the forms and stayed out of trouble without them.

To Lorraine May - for legal advice that pulled me back from the brink several times.

To Catherine Knepper who, by applying her talent and editing skills, helped me to understand how to make stories come alive.

To Dick Gibson an early friend and editor who asked questions that clarified what I was attempting to say.

To John Regan and Bob Fretz, who took the time to answer questions, to read manuscripts and to offer suggestions for the accuracy of the substance and of my memories.

To our family—Kent, Kim, Kelsey, Kallen, Karsen and Kennedy, and Krista and Scott Hartman—for unqualified love and support throughout this great adventure. You thought I could do it - and you made me believe it too!

SPECIAL NOTE TO BOOK CLUB READERS

If your book club chooses to collectively read "More Than A Walk on the Beach," I would really enjoy having a discussion with the group. Please contact me at ambassadormkramer@gmail.com so we can set a mutually convenient time. I look forward to hearing from you.

MY DEDICATION

To Kay—my life partner, my best friend
and my trusted guide—for encouraging me
to take risks and accept challenges, and
supporting me while I did...

TABLE OF CONTENTS

MORE THAN A WALK ON THE BEACH

I've never needed a vacation like I did in the spring of 2003. I was President of the Iowa State Senate, and the 2003 legislative session was one of the most contentious I'd witnessed in over a decade of public service. Budget shortfalls in Medicaid and other human services programs had everyone's nerves on a high boil. Democrats were accusing Republicans of not caring about the poor, Republicans were accusing Democrats of not caring about how much money was spent, and our discourse had descended to name-calling and mudslinging. Even when we managed to speak politely to each other in public, Politician A would then race to the media to be sure his or her spin would be seen and heard before Politician B. It was every individual for themselves. We were behaving like petty, mean-spirited adolescents, and worse, all the squabbling and acrimony prevented us from accomplishing much of anything. It was the third year of my fourth four-year term as a state senator, my sixth year as president, and I *knew* I wasn't going to run again.

But another full year stood between me and retirement, and it was high time for a vacation. My husband Kay and I flew off to Hilton Head Island for a much needed week of lounging on the beach, reading, and golf. We landed in Savannah, Georgia, claimed the luggage, and loaded our rental car. I couldn't wait to plant myself on the beach and leave that legislative battlefield far behind. Driving away from the airport, I could feel myself unwinding. Then I turned on my cell phone. Message alerts began beeping and flashing—three voicemails, each increasingly frantic, "Call Becky." Becky was my administrative assistant in the Senate President's office and I loved her dearly, but I really did not want to speak to her.

So I did what any dedicated public servant would do. I procrastinated.

I acted as navigator while Kay drove us to our condominium. I admired the scenery. I wondered aloud what the kids and grandkids were doing. I looked through the contents of my purse. I read through the fine print on our rental car agreement. Anything to avoid making that call.

When we arrived at our destination, I was barely inside the lobby door when the young woman at the desk accosted me.

"Senator Kramer, we have an urgent message for you. Call Becky immediately!"

Duty fulfilled, she slumped behind the desk in obvious relief. Meanwhile I fought a wave of panic—Becky wouldn't go to such lengths to find me unless something was really wrong. Someone was sick, or had died, or perhaps there'd been an accident.

Guilt drove me straight up to our condo so I could make the call from the porch.

"Mary, I've been trying to reach you for hours!" Becky said. "You need to call the White House."

What? All the drama for this. Calls from the White House usually just meant we could expect a visit from someone in the administration – probably in the next few days. And by that time it was after six p.m. on the East Coast, and a Friday night no less. No one would be there.

"Sure thing, Becky," I said. "I'll call them first thing Monday." "*No, Mary. They are waiting for your call – you have to do it now!*" With an apologetic look at Kay, I agreed – "OK, OK, I'm calling right now."

"White House Personnel" answered. Whoa, this was new. I identified myself and the woman on the line got right to it. "Senator Kramer, we've been waiting for your call," she said. "The president would like to know if you would consider serving as the United States Ambassador to Barbados."

I sat down, hard, in the nearest chair.

"You must not speak to anyone about this except your immediate family," she said. "No one but your husband and children. The president would like you to call back at three p.m. on Monday with your answer. Are you willing to consider it?"

The chair I'd fallen onto was a lovely shade of green, emblazoned with flowers and butterflies. It was a beautiful, warm evening in May. I could hear the surf and the birds. I could see vacationers strolling up and down the beach, swimmers getting in a last dip before dinner. Funny how you remember this stuff.

These details raised to the forefront of my mind, crowding out everything, even the ability to think, move, or speak. "Senator Kramer?" the woman said. "Are you still there?"

I can't quite remember what I said when I finally dragged myself out of that paralyzed state. I think (I hope) I said, "I'm really honored, and I'll consider it."

"Wonderful," she said. "The president will expect to hear from you on Monday." She hung up.

I just sat there, holding onto the phone and the chair for dear life. Kay joined me on the porch. He took one look at me and said, "What's wrong with you? Are you sick?"

I had regained my power of speech, but I still couldn't move. I just stared at the tumbling Atlantic, totally indifferent to my plight. "No, not sick."

"Well for chrissakes, Mary, what is it? Did something terrible happen?"

"President Bush wants me to consider being an ambassador."

Suddenly Kay was speechless, too. We just stared at each other.

I don't know how much time passed before we regained our faculties. But when we did, questions followed in a torrent. What would be involved in the process? Were we willing to move out of the country, away from friends and family? Was I willing to put off retirement? And a more pertinent question: What exactly did an ambassador do?

President Bush had been wonderfully generous with his time in Iowa helping us raise money for state legislative candidates, even attending an event at our home. But this. Totally unexpected and way over the top!

Finally Kay, ever practical, came up with a suggestion that cut through all the fog. "Let's go to Barnes and Noble, get a book, and at least figure out where the hell Barbados is."

At a cramped table in the bookstore café, we sipped lattés and huddled over The Adventurer's Guide to Barbados. After a few minutes of reading about white-sand beaches, turquoise waters, amazing food, and the relaxed island culture, Kay said, "How tough can this be? It has definite possibilities." We bought the book and headed immediately back to our condo to call our son and daughter, Kent and Krista.

"Kent," I said, "what do you think of your mother as a U.S. Ambassador to Barbados, perhaps living out of the country for several years?"

Kent, always the thoughtful son, replied, "Gosh, Mom, what an honor. You'd make a great ambassador. You should definitely say yes. And hey, do you think you'll be there in time for Christmas?"

Obviously he knew where Barbados was.

Krista, always ready for action, was even more enthusiastic. "Wow, Mom, this really kicks ass!" she said. "Go for it."

And then, the most important opinion. "Kay," I said, "what do you think?"

"I think we should go to dinner."

There's a reason I've been married to this man for over fifty years.

By the time appetizers were served Kay had collected his thoughts. "Here's what I'm thinking," he said. "We don't know what your duties would be, whether we get paid, how long we might be away, where we would live, or what hoops we have to jump through to even get this job. How can we decide right now? We need more information."

He was right, of course. These were critical questions and we had no answers, and that fearsome list didn't even speak to the questions running through my mind. Did I have the skills for the job? Did I want to uproot everything, delay retirement, and be away from family and friends for years? Did I really want to stay in the political limelight? Most important, would I be able to actually make a difference? To make a radical life change like this, I needed to know I wasn't going to be just a ribbon-cutter or a glorified hostess, no matter how beautiful the surroundings.

By the time we finished dinner, Kay and I had a long list of questions, and as there was no one to ask until Monday, we agreed that we would just not think about it. And that's exactly what we did. We enjoyed a long, relaxing weekend, experiencing the life we hoped to live in retirement: reading, playing golf, walking the beach, relishing not being scheduled.

Inevitably, however, three p.m. on Monday rolled around. I still wasn't sure what I'd do. On the phone with the White House Personnel person I tried to be, dare I say it, diplomatic.

"I'm so honored to be asked to do this," I said, "but you know, I have no idea what's expected of ambassadors. I need to do something meaningful—at least have the opportunity to make a difference. I really don't want to go there just to attend parties and cut ribbons."

"Could you hold a minute?" the woman on the phone replied.

There was a pause and then a click. "I understand you have some questions, Mary?"

The voice was unmistakable. It was the President of the United States.

I babbled something about wanting to make a real difference and wanting to be more than a ribbon cutter, and President Bush broke in. "Mary," he said, "I'm not sending you there for a walk on the beach. We need some of that Iowa common sense down there, right now."

"Yes, sir," I blurted. "We'll do it. Thank you for your confidence in me."

I hung up and Kay and I looked at each other.

"What have we done?" I said.

Thus began my adventures as a United States ambassador, a rare privilege for anyone, perhaps especially for a girl from Iowa whose father worried she couldn't even hold a job.

CHAPTER ONE

AN INVITATION TO PARADISE...EVENTUALLY

We settled in to our lovely condo, went to the grocery store, walked the beach, enjoyed breakfasts on our patio, and scheduled our golf outings. Of course we made a list of all the favorite haunts where we must go—especially for dinner.

It immediately became apparent that this was going to be anything but an apolitical vacation. Within the hour, faxes began arriving from the White House, fast and furious. The front desk people were awestruck.

So were we. We spent the first few days of our vacation fielding faxes and giddily, though with some trepidation, pondering what we were getting into. At some point I noted the irony of my restorative getaway: As intended, I had forgotten entirely about the political brouhaha back in Iowa, but only because I now had all new political brouhaha to consider.

So we enjoyed our time, reading, golfing, walking the beach, and enjoying the delightful restaurants on Hilton Head. As always, it seemed our time was too short and it was time to pack up and return home.

Once there, the paperwork blizzard began in earnest. FedEx was at our door almost daily for weeks. The multitude of forms to be completed would ultimately become a 14-inch stack—I know because I measured it. After the first delivery, we began to review the information we would need to provide, and we realized that nothing about us would ever be confidential again.

We were asked to list our family trees, everywhere we'd lived, everywhere we had gone to school, every organization we were a part of, everywhere we'd worked. We were asked to provide names and addresses of people who could vouch for us at each of these stops in our lives. Since we were still not allowed to tell anyone of our potential nomination, none of these folks knew we were naming them.

A full medical review and subsequent report was required for both of us, including our HIV/AIDS status. No confidentiality here. And, were we up to date on our shots? Happily, yes.

We listed every board we'd ever served on and described every leadership position in any organization we'd held for the last five years. Enough already!

But no, it wasn't. It took us nearly three months to complete all the forms for the White House and the State Department, and just when we thought we were off the hook, the paperwork for the Senate Foreign Relations Committee began arriving. These forms demanded full financial disclosure, including all our investments and all changes in our portfolio for the past five years. We were asked to list the dollar amounts in all our bank accounts and, finally, to provide the sources and amounts of our income for the past five years. Without the assistance of our financial advisors at the Foster Group, we would never have been able to provide all that with any degree of accuracy.

We were also asked to list every political contribution we, our parents, and our children and their spouses had made for the past five years.

Obviously, the senators required more disclosure from us than they require of themselves.

The final set of forms asked for the names, addresses, and phone numbers of twenty-five people who were not named anywhere else in the paperwork and who could vouch for us. And there was still the caveat: We could under no circumstances let them know they were on the list. By that time we were getting down to listing business colleagues and new neighbors, and even checking our Christmas card list.

"What have you gotten us into?" Kay asked. It was a question he would pose repeatedly during the lengthy eight-month confirmation process, and even more emphatically after we'd left the United States.

Meantime, since we could not discuss any of these developments with anyone, we found ourselves living a strange dual life. It was hard not to be con-sumed with the ambassadorship, but we had to carry on as if everything were normal. The sheer busyness of our lives made it easier. My schedule was full. I made calls to raise campaign funds for Senate colleagues, travelled around the state speaking about the legislative sessions to civic groups, supporting my colleagues at their fund raising events, and enjoying our granddaughters' recitals and soccer games. Kay was busy with his consulting clients, his boards, and his golf game.

In mid-August, with Iowa's temperatures in the 90s, a State Department diplomatic security agent arrived in Des Moines. He called me on my cell phone while I was attending a fundraising luncheon, introduced himself as a State Department Security Agent, and asked me to meet with him at my home in thirty minutes. As I was to be the luncheon speaker, I told him it would take at least an hour for me to get there. He was pleasantly agreeable. "No problem, Senator," he said. "I'll see you there at your convenience." When I asked if he needed directions to my house he demurred. "I know exactly where you live, Ms. Kramer," he said. Of course he did…what was I thinking? I learned during our meeting he had come to Iowa to conduct interviews with my "list of twenty-five," the friends and neighbors I'd listed on my forms.

And as he soon learned, our friends were a protective lot, and tended to be a bit cranky and uncooperative.

The agent was a white haired man in a dark suit and tie, wearing dark framed glasses and carrying a briefcase. On a sweltering day in August, he approached one of our neighbors as he walked down his driveway to his mail-box. The agent flashed his badge and asked the neighbor if he knew me. "Let me see that badge again, buddy," our neighbor said. Later, he told us that he was afraid the IRS was after us. Other friends didn't answer their front doors, so the agent simply walked around to their back yard, and if he found them there, he began asking questions. Mostly they ended up interviewing him first. Almost everyone he contacted insisted on speaking to Kay or me before they would answer his questions. Our phones were busy with friends asking us what was going on and if we needed help. Rumors were flying.

And still we could not confirm or deny anything. "Just answer the questions," we said. "We're not in trouble. We'll fill you in as soon as we can."

Then, at a few of the later interviews, the agent let the cat out of the bag. He asked if so-and-so knew of any reason I shouldn't be named an ambassador. The news didn't take long to get out. Des Moines is a small town at heart and Kay and I were well known. A few days later some friends told us they were on the golf course and heard another friend shout across the fairway "What's the deal about Mary Kramer being an ambassador? Have you talked to this State Department security guy? Who is he anyway? Should we be talking to him? Do Mary and Kay know what he's up to?"

We might as well have taken out an ad on the front page of the Des Moines Register.

Finally, in early September, after a lengthy review of our paperwork and assiduous reference checking, the official announcement from the White House appeared on the State Department website. Even though ambassadors report directly to the president, the Department of State (DOS) makes the official announcements regarding embassies. "President George W. Bush announces his intention to nominate Mary Kramer of Iowa as the United States Ambassador Extraordinary and Plenipotentiary to Barbados and the nations of the Eastern Caribbean." My jaw dropped. For the first time I realized I would be working with seven nations, not just one. The embassy located in Bridgetown serves not only Barbados, but six other Eastern Caribbean countries as well.

Kay stared alternately at the computer screen and me. "What have you gotten us into?"

Later, I learned that I was the only ambassador in the world to be assigned to represent the United States to so many governments. The countries were small to be sure, but there were still seven of them: Barbados, Grenada, Antigua and Barbuda, St. Lucia, St. Vincent and the Grenadines, Dominica, and St. Kitts and Nevis. And they all expected and were deserving of our attention. We're talking seven different governments, seven different cultures, seven different histories, seven different sets of administrative and diplomatic duties, and a combined population of over 800,000. What, indeed, had I gotten us into?

With the White House announcement officially made, we were finally free to speak publicly about the job's possibilities and our enthusiasm for it, even though it was still a long road to confirmation. We were told to begin every conversation with "*If* we are confirmed..." The United States Senate takes its prerogative of confirmation very seriously, and an ambassadorial appointment was never a sure thing. I learned of several examples of failed confirmations. One in particular involved an appointee to Barbados and the Eastern Caribbean. Apparently, the nominee simply assumed approval, and immediately after the White House announcement, rented a house, moved to Barbados and started work. That individual was NOT confirmed...

Locally, we were an immediate media sensation. Reporters, photographers, and TV news people all wanted to talk about our "exciting possibilities." Everyone was thrilled to have a hometown girl in such a role—there had been few ambassadors from Iowa. After years of being in politics, I was accustomed to being in the public eye, but this was a spotlight on full glare.

I wouldn't be in Iowa for long. Immediately after the White House announcement, consultations began in earnest. Many trips to Washington would occur before confirmation.

The DOS organization divides the world into five separate bureaus, and mine was Western Hemisphere Affairs (WHA). Managing the ambassadorial consultation-and-learning process was the responsibility of WHA. A primary part of that job was to determine what consultations would be appropriate and necessary, and then schedule appointments. There was such high turnover in WHA that during my consultation process, four different people had a role in scheduling and accompanying me to meetings. Nonetheless, they managed to schedule meetings for me to meet with each of the U.S. bureaus, departments, and agencies represented at Embassy Bridgetown or in the Caribbean. Every federal agency represented at the American Embassy in Bridgetown, Barbados, wanted to speak to me. So for the next three months, with many flights back and forth from Iowa, Kay and I were in Washington. We stayed at a small, quirky hotel, the State Plaza Hotel, within walking distance to the State Department. It consisted mostly of suites that had been decorated in the 1950s—lots of pastel pinks and blues. Our suite was quite roomy and included a kitchenette right out of *Leave it to Beaver*. It did, however, have a microwave. We became quite adept at creating meals from food available at the nearby convenience store. Breakfast cereal and orange juice, frozen dinners, and microwave popcorn became staples in our diet. We also learned to enjoy "takeout" from the DOS employee food court.

The consultations were intended to familiarize me with the mission of each of the agencies represented at the embassy, but they also gave the people in Washington a chance to look me over and to fill my ears with what they thought was important. I listened carefully, took notes, and then asked each agency or department leader what they expected from an ambassador in support of their mission. I was checking on them as well. Meanwhile, the WHA "handler," who accompanied me everywhere I went, was also taking notes. I never learned why that note taking was so important. Was I being rated on my performance, or did some WHA staffer "higher up" need to know what was being said? Or perhaps it just helped them to stay awake during the long conversations. Asking about hopes or expectations of the agencies seemed an obvious question for an ambassador-in-training to pose, but a curious thing happened. Each time I asked the question, I was met with a look of bemusement or wonder—one woman's jaw dropped in a cartoon parody of shock. And there were no pat answers forthcoming. Apparently it was not the "done" thing for the potential ambassador to ask questions.

"Just ask your DCM," was the most common answer. The Deputy Chief of Mission (DCM) is second in command to the ambassador and is always a career Foreign Service officer with a wealth of institutional knowledge. My DCM would've been the perfect person to ask, but he or she wasn't in Washington, and at that point I didn't even know who he or she was. Others vaguely referred me to someone "higher up" in the department. Perhaps the agency or bureau leaders had been instructed not to answer my questions, but I don't think so. The more likely explanation is that they actually didn't have answers. They didn't expect to need answers.

The same thing happened at my visits to the various departments and bureaus within DOS. I spent time with leaders in the Pentagon, the Federal Bureau of Investigation (FBI), and the United States Agency for International Development (USAID), the Drug Enforcement Agency (DEA), and the Department of the Treasury and the Department of Commerce, among others. The stated purpose of each visit was to inform me of that agency or department's mission and goals for the embassy. The goal of the individual representatives however, was almost always crystal clear. They needed to convince me that theirs was the *most important* work of the embassy and deserved the ambassador's full attention and support. At the end of most interviews, I asked my usual questions. How could the ambassador help accomplish the agency goals? How did the agency goals fit with the embassy goals? What were the embassy's goals. Again the department representatives were not comfortable answering. Again I got the referral to someone "higher up."

For instance, coming out of a meeting with USAID in which we discussed the importance of trade to the folks in the Caribbean and some of the initiatives underway, I asked, "What can the ambassador do to move the agenda forward?" I got a vague response about hoping I understood that funding was becoming scarce and positions were being relocated, ending with a hope that I would be able to have an impact in spite of some of the negatives. I pressed on: "What negatives? What positions? Should I expect staffing or funding changes?" No one was forthcoming with answers. As I was to learn, this was often the DOS *modus operandi*. Communication with the field was not a high priority. If I wanted answers, I would have to find them on my own. Certainly, I learned some things about all these groups, but if I wanted practical information about budgets or staffing, issues or even potential projects, it would have to be on-the-job.

It took me a while to figure out what was at work here. The answer: Two words: *political appointee*. It's no secret that appointments are often given as political rewards, usually for a role played during a campaign or in recognition of a key relationship with the president. As such, we political appointees are an admittedly motley bunch. Many have excelled in their chosen fields but are ill-suited for an ambassadorial position in terms of education, experience, or skills. A few political appointees have failed conspicuously and terribly; some have been merely ineffective. But the large majority have been carefully selected for their expertise related to their assignment; bringing a wealth of experience, new expertise, and fresh air to stifling bureaucracies. So even though protocol was always followed to a "T," everyone at the State Department was polite, deferential, and even solicitous, it wasn't difficult to see that as a group, DOS staffers viewed political appointees as incompetent nuts requiring careful handling. You might have been a macadamia nut as opposed to a walnut, but you were still a nut.

Nutty or not, I was disappointed that individual qualifications and experience weren't taken into consideration. The stereotype of the political appointee prevailed. I suppose it's somewhat understandable since the ambassador position is the top of the career pyramid for Foreign Service professionals and political appointees fill those positions—limiting upward mobility for some. For the first time in a long time, I felt my credibility and the value of my life experience were in question, and it did not sit well with me. I guess I shouldn't have been surprised that the State Department treated us with kid gloves, but I resented the somewhat patronizing "Don't you worry your pretty little head" response to my questions and the "Just ask your DCM" response which gave me the impression that the judgment had been made that I was incompetent and unqualified. I had years of leadership and management experience before I entered politics. I determined then and there to demonstrate my ability and skill to do the job. Apparently the President of the United States thought I was qualified.

In October, Kay and I attended a two-week Ambassadorial Seminar presented by the Foreign Service Institute (FSI), which is the training institution for the DOS. This seminar is known affectionately, at least within the Foreign Service community, as "Charm School."

Our Charm School class of ambassadorial candidates was a combination of professional career Foreign Service officers and political appointees. Everyone had been announced by the White House as a nominee, but otherwise we were at different stages in the confirmation process. It was a fascinating group of people with an astounding array of experience. Oil company executives, international bankers, world-famous art collectors, philanthropists, key policy makers from branches of government and Foreign Service professionals who had served all over the world. Kay and I felt a little like sparrows in a room full of peacocks, but we found enough in common with our classmates that we made some good friends. Many of them became helpful resources on the job, and we continue to enjoy friendships with a number of those folks to this day.

The curriculum of Charm School was fascinating, both for what it covered and what it did not. One full morning was dedicated to explaining the organizational chart of the State Department. Acronyms were so plentiful it felt like we were learning a new language, and the number of layers of management and supervision was mind-boggling. Multinational corporations don't have nearly as many management levels as the DOS. Absorbing all the data was like trying to drink from a fire hose. Another morning was spent watching Power

Point explanations of the bureaucratic rules we would be expected to follow—
a style of meeting I later learned was called "death by Power Point" by the
military. We spent another entire afternoon learning the expense reporting
and record-keeping requirements of the job. Bureaucracy diligently at work.
Frankly, it was a struggle for me to find the relevance in this amount of detail,
or to see the value of so much time spent on something that could've been
covered in a handout. If I wanted information or had questions, I knew I could
question people at my embassy and they would assist me. Teaching me where
to seek data when needed surely would have been less time-consuming and
more relevant.

Our instructors paid particular attention to the proper division of public
and private expenses at the ambassadorial residence. We were told that the
rules required that an ambassador use personal funds to pay all entertainment, catering, liquor, and decorating bills. An expense report would then be
submitted, which would likely be paid after thirty days. One of our classmates
raised his hand. He'd been told that entertainment expenses could reach the
tens of thousands of dollars. "And this is money the ambassador fronts?" he
asked. He was told, yes, expenses could be that high and yes, the ambassador
is expected to pay up front and in addition, and any errors or submissions
viewed as outside the rules could subject us to federal investigation for fraud.
A minor uproar ensued, and our vocal classmate's consternation could be
heard over the din: "These procedures are not only stupid, they're immoral!"
Another gentleman spoke up and said "I understand we need to buy our own
corn flakes but this is ridiculous!" Of course, nothing changed. Sure enough,
throughout our years of service, Kay and I were required to pay entertainment
bills up front and then submit them for reimbursement. The only entertainment expenses allowed were for entertaining local citizens or visitors from
other countries. If at least half the group we were entertaining was American,
the ambassador paid all expenses personally. This was true whether we were
entertaining at public venues or at the residence.

We were told we were going to receive a salary–although it wasn't quite
clear what "step" of the salary schedule we would be on. Later that evening
(over yet another Lean Cuisine and a bottle of wine from the CVS) Kay and I
discussed what we had learned so far and set a goal for ourselves. We would
try to live within our means. We would use all the funds we had allocated for
retirement income at home, add whatever salary we received, and try to come
out even. At the end of our tour, we did not meet our goal, but we might have if
it were it not for plane tickets when we needed to make home visits.

We now had a lot of information on organization charts, money and rules,
but information about the issues we would be expected to present to heads
of government was almost entirely missing. Again, bureaucracy diligently

at work. For instance, deportation was a big, controversial issue all over the world. A discussion involving the reasons deportees are returned to their home countries, the process for doing so, and how to approach the issue with government officials and the local media would have been extremely helpful.

Another glaring omission. Silly me, I thought a new ambassador should arrive at Post fully briefed on the significant issues of their countries, yet not a word was spoken about the cultural, social, or political situations of our individual posts. It is true that different countries and regions often have unique issues. But there are many common issues where information and suggested approaches to government officials would have been helpful. Discussion that involved some of the divisive issues of the day worldwide, and sharing approaches that had been successful (best practices) would have gone a long way toward preparing me to hit the ground running.

Thankfully, two active ambassadors—career diplomat Ambassador Jimmy Kolker, then-ambassador to Uganda, and political appointee Ambassador Sue Cobb, then-ambassador to Jamaica—arrived on the scene. Their descriptions of their work days and their successes and challenges were among the most relevant and useful information we received. Ambassador Prudence Bushnell was serving as U.S. Ambassador to Kenya when the embassy there was bombed in 1998, killing several Americans and injuring many others. Ambassador Bushnell led several wonderful and meaningful discussions about the role of the ambassador as leader of both policy and personnel in the embassy. Small in stature, she was a strong, articulate woman who did not equivocate about the depth and breadth of the position we would be undertaking. "You will be expected to take responsibility for *everything* that happens in your embassy," she told us. Listening to her helped me to understand the importance of the role of the ambassador and that the buck definitely stopped with me.

During Charm School I continued to struggle with the bias against politically appointed ambassadors. I could feel the caution Foreign Service officers exercised while they were working with us. Doubts were always very subtle, never voiced, and the official protocol and the proper titles were always in place. But when I had questions, I got the "company" line: "Just ask your DCM." I suspected that the curriculum was designed to make sure that politically appointed ambassadors would find themselves dependent on the Deputy Chief of Mission. Political appointees weren't to be trusted—in a few cases I will admit, with good reason. Still, I guess I had hoped for more respect for my motivation to serve and for my experience.

Meanwhile, Kay was struggling a bit as well. While I was having my questions dodged, he, along with two other men, found himself in a spouse-of-ambassadorial-appointees program with twenty plus wives. Kay is an old hand at being the male spouse of a public official and learned to enjoy the role. He had the self-confidence and sense of humor to join the spouse organization of the Iowa Legislature, even though it was called the Ladies Legislative League. After he joined, they began referring to it as the LLL in his honor. In Charm School, he gamely endured tips on managing the household staff, entertaining ideas (Easter Egg hunts and Trick or Treat parties), keeping track of food expenses, and "fork counting" (yes, we literally had to count every utensil and make a record of it). He was carefully working toward graduating from Charm School without making any waves, until the presenters suggested that the ambassadorial spouse should invite the wives of prime ministers and foreign ministers to lunch or tea at the residence as a gesture of friendship. Kay raised his hand. "I'm not sure all prime ministers or foreign ministers would look too kindly on the idea of me inviting their wives to tea." For a moment the instructors were stumped. Neither of them knew what to say, and the room was filled with laughter. They took a moment to consult, and then announced that yes, such a gesture from him might be misunderstood and inappropriate. Kay graciously agreed with them.

I think he made some comment about having them over for a beer and a ball game before he let the matter drop...

During week two of the seminar, we attended a day-long security seminar at FSI, where we were warned about terrorism, kidnappings of Americans, and other security considerations. I am not prone to anxiety, but with the examples provided, I realized it was really only common sense to follow all the security conditions and protections we were provided. It was also made clear we would always be under some sort of surveillance. It was highly likely someone would always be watching, friend or foe. Not too different from serving in political office. There are always people watching who would like to "catch" you doing something inappropriate. Even if it was just going to the grocery store in shorts and a t-shirt.

Charm School certainly wasn't all bad. It provided ample opportunity to learn what was expected by the bureaucracy and by each department at DOS. I gained a clear understanding of the pecking order on the organization chart of the DOS and the embassy, and I learned more than I ever wanted to know about processes for filing expense reports, time and attendance forms, requisitioning and budgeting, and so on and so on. The opportunity to get to know our colleagues and appreciate all their talents was invaluable.

The FSI training staff is good at their jobs and each one of them earned my respect throughout the session. The deficiencies in curriculum could be easily corrected if the trainers were free to develop curricula based on feedback from people in the field. That would require in depth collection and analysis of feed-back from the participants, but the effort might be extremely valuable.

Ready or not, at the end of the two weeks, even Charm School's most diffi-cult students were deemed to have passed. Kay showed off his certificate with great pride and declared that he was officially qualified not to invite people to tea. It was the end of October and we wondered how many more trips to Washington there would be. Even though we were racking up the frequent flyer miles, the trips back and forth were expensive.

Meanwhile, I was being prepared for the "murder board," a rite-of-passage interview intended to prepare a candidate for the Senate Foreign Relations Committee (SFRC) hearings. This "board" was described to me as a group of people engaged in a broad and diverse range of policy areas in the DOS who would fire questions at me and aggressively challenge my answers. It sounded awful, but I was actually looking forward to it. My legislative experi-ence had forced me to articulate positions on controversial issues, so I was anticipating a lively discussion, and I do love a challenge.

But the murder board turned out to be nothing like advertised. Many questions were asked over the two-hour period, but it seemed as if the members of the board viewed the session as an opportunity to explain their own positions and opinions. Only sometimes did these monologues include a question. I sat back and listened. And listened and listened. For my part I was asked basic, fact-based questions about the Caribbean, i.e., When do the countries have elections? Who are the major political players? My responses must have been appropriate because they were never challenged. It was kind of like the fifth grade when the teacher expected us to memorize and recite the capitals of the fifty states.

My testimony before the Senate Foreign Relations Committee was another new and memorable experience. To prepare, I visited with or called members of the Iowa Congressional Delegation, asking for their support. Members on both sides of the aisle were very gracious and assured me of their support. They all indicated it was a great thing for Iowa to have an ambassador and offered whatever help they or their staff members could provide.

It was a different lesson when I met with the SFRC staff members for a pre-hearing discussion, something of a dry run before the hearing itself. As usual, my DOS handlers accompanied me, always taking notes.

Senator Christopher Dodd's Chief of Staff asked the first question, and it set the tone: "How much did *you* pay to get this job?" I was so tempted to respond "None of your business!" but I fell back on my politically correct, end-lessly pleasant mode and said, "I completed every form required, and I'm sure you know the amount of every political contribution we made. Surely we can agree this job is worth more than that!"

Another congressional staffer said, "Don't get too comfortable down there, because you won't be there long. We're going to beat Bush next year." *Hmmmm, I thought, we'll see.* But I just smiled and responded "Anything's possible."

These folks are bright and likable human beings under most circumstances, and my political experience helped me to understand that politics can create unhappy, angry, and negative people. But sometimes this type of mean spirited partisanship interferes with duty. The power attached to staffers' jobs is directly related to the majority or minority status of their boss. The minority status does not include getting to make appointments. So, nothing personal, it goes with the territory.

Even so, I was completely taken off guard by the next question: "Are you prepared to clean up the mess your predecessor left behind?"

Mess? No one had spoken to me about any messes. I only knew it had been several months since a U.S. ambassador had been on location in Barbados. So I responded truthfully but generally: "I am confident I am capable of dealing with whatever problems and issues I will face."

Out of the corner of my eye I glanced at my State Department handlers. They had come to attention and were on the edges of their chairs. Oops... What was going on? Perhaps I was a little too emphatic. Or was I too vague? Had the committee been expecting me to be able to address the issues my predecessor left behind, or lay out a strategy for cleaning up? I could do neither. I risked a quick glance at Kay. He gave me a meaningful look and I knew exactly what he was thinking. By then he didn't even need to voice the "What have you gotten us into?" question.

No one wanted to discuss it on the way back to DOS either. Not even an "Ask your DCM."

By late fall the actual Foreign Relations Committee hearing and vote on my confirmation still hadn't occurred. I was back in Washington for more consultations, and during that time I was extremely fortunate to be invited to a two-day conference for current American ambassadors from across Latin and South America and the Caribbean. The conference was sponsored by the Assistant Secretary of State for WHA. I attended as an observer, and it was a fantastic opportunity. I was able to listen to current ambassadors, both career and political, describe the state of affairs in their countries and the degree of difficulty of presenting specific issues to government leaders. These firsthand accounts from people who were doing the very work I was about to undertake enhanced my learning exponentially. I began to understand exactly what had to be done and something about the degree of difficulty and potential confrontational nature of my tasks.

And along with all my new knowledge came self-doubt. I knew I had reached the level of conscious incompetence. *I understood how much I did not know.* My salvation came in the form of Deputy Chief of Mission (DCM) Marcia Bernicat, the official conference representative from Embassy Bridgetown. DCM Bernicat was immediately distinguishable from the rest of the attendees because before her on the table there was not just one, but seven flags—a veritable bouquet. It was another visceral reminder of how complex this job was going to be and how great my responsibility was. During the first break she rushed over to meet me and tell me how happy she was to work with someone with my experience. That was just so helpful to me.

Later that afternoon, Marcia and I managed to find a couple of hours to have a glass of wine and get acquainted. A wonderful, gifted woman, Marcia is a tall, beautiful, smart, articulate woman with a wealth of experience at DOS. At one of her postings she adopted two young boys. Part of the conversation included me learning something about what it was like for her to manage two small boys and a dog in a new country. Impressive. A single mother running a family and an embassy. Marcia had been heading up the embassy in Bridgetown for many months since my predecessor left. It had occurred to me that she might find me superfluous—after all, she had been doing the job single-handedly for months. Instead, she was warm and welcoming, and made it obvious she was happy to work with me—she had read my resume and told me she was sure I could be very effective. She also explained why she believed it was critical for these small Caribbean countries to have an ambassador in residence as the president's representative. Without that level of leadership in place, the small countries felt that the U.S. was ignoring them and disrespecting their sovereignty. We had a great conversation about a shared vision of the desired future and what we might accomplish together. I asked her to describe the state of relationships with our various governments as well as her own goals and aspirations. She provided a succinct and useful sketch of each country and the relationships with their governments. Some good and some not so good. To use a trite term, we bonded that afternoon and joked about being sisters in another life. I truly felt blessed to find a compatible, smart woman who would not only be my colleague but would also be my friend. Her description and analysis of the state of affairs at the embassy and the relationship with our seven countries provided a solid foundation for my early job performance. We made an aggressive schedule for my arrival and beyond. We talked about how I would approach the employees at the Embassy and the importance of a social schedule to begin making friends. We agreed I would attempt to present credentials to all seven governments within my

first six weeks at Post—demonstrating a high energy approach. I'll always be grateful for the trust she placed in me that afternoon, and for her candid and professional review of current conditions. My doubts began to dissolve.
I could "Ask my DCM." Like "the little engine that could," I thought I could. And I started to believe I could do this job.

Around noon on the second day of the conference, I got a wonderful surprise: The call came informing me that the Senate Foreign Relations Committee had called hearings, and I would be on at three o'clock that afternoon. My DOS handlers picked me up and rushed me off to give testimony in the Senate Office Building. The room was historic and beautiful, with white marble walls, deep red carpeting, and a raised dais for members of the committee, with chairs for their staff behind them. If I hadn't been in awe of the process before, entering that room provided that feeling.

Two other nominees (one for Peru and one for the International Bank) also were being interviewed that afternoon, and so the green felt-covered table where we were to sit was adorned with three leather folders and three crystal glasses, three crystal pitchers of ice water. Three large, high-backed black leather swivel chairs on casters were placed behind the table facing the dais where the senators sat, their staff members behind them. As senators and staff filed in, we were escorted to our places at the table.

After being seated in that huge chair I realized that unless I perched on the very front edge, my feet wouldn't touch the floor. And unless I sat very still, the chair tilted backward and the casters rolled unpredictably on the marble floor. I feared if I moved at all I might find myself sprawled on the floor before the Committee. I began to make a plan about waving to them as I fell to the floor and slid under the table (not a comforting thought). The hearing was about to be called to order, so it was too late to do anything but clutch the edge of the table and hope for the best. Talk about being frozen in place!

Senator Norm Coleman from Minnesota chaired the hearing that day. This was fortunate for me, as we had met several times back in the Midwest. He began by saying how refreshing it was to have someone from Iowa who could bring that great Hawkeye spirit (he was a graduate of the University of Iowa Law School) and Midwest common sense to the job. His presence and demeanor eased my nerves considerably. I was sure he would come down and pick me up if I fell off my chair.

After all three of us had delivered our opening prepared statements, Senator Dodd came into the room. He sat down and, looking primarily at me, delivered a lengthy speech about how poorly President Bush was handling diplomatic relations in the Caribbean—never providing enough people or money—and how he hoped there would be significant change after the next election. Then, Senator Dodd fixed his gaze on me. "You are apparently very close to the president," he said. "Tell him what I said." Then he left the room. I really wanted to remind him that the budget for the people and the money to support programs are the province of Congress. Fortunately, there was no opportunity for me to respond.

We were excused after completing our remarks and answering questions. Later that afternoon the Committee voted unanimously in favor of our confirmations, and our names were placed on the docket for the vote of the full Senate. But when would *that* vote take place? Most people were betting that it wouldn't be scheduled until after the Christmas recess.

So, next morning, resigned to yet another delay, I returned to Iowa, still not confirmed. We enjoyed Thanksgiving with our family—everyone wondering what was next—when would we be leaving?

In early November, Kay and I had received an exciting invitation to attend the White House Christmas party. This was an opportunity of a lifetime, and we decided to go. How many people get to visit the White House? Pretty special for two Iowans. So in early December we returned to Washington to attend the party. The White House is a venerable and beautiful setting, and President and Mrs. Bush were most gracious as host and hostess. I couldn't help but think of Laura during the campaign. I had been one of the early supporters of their candidacy and later on during the 2000 campaign I became the statewide campaign chair. That allowed Kay and me to meet and visit with then-Governor and Mrs. Bush several times at various campaign events. In February of the previous year, we hosted a reception for Laura in Des Moines. This was simply an opportunity for her to do a solo event and meet many of her and her husband's supporters. She was visibly nervous beforehand, and as I stood with her in the receiving line, from time to time I squeezed her hand in a gesture of support. Of course, she was her usual gracious self and the event was a great success. It has been thrilling for me to observe her in her role as an effective, gracious, articulate and beloved public figure. A woman who has served our country well and achieved much. And that night at the White House Christmas Party, she was completely at ease and in her element.

As President and Mrs. Bush and Vice President and Mrs. Cheney came down the red-carpeted stairway, President Bush spotted Kay and me. He came over to greet us and said, "Mary, haven't they confirmed you yet? We need you to get underway down there." It was a staggering thing to realize the President of the United States knew our names and the progress of our confirmation process.

Later that same evening, Karl Rove, the president's chief political advisor, greeted us. He really enjoyed referring to me as "Madame President" and did so at every opportunity. So he shouted across the room "Madam President, are you confirmed?" and said, "Shall I call you Madam Ambassador?" If only!

As in nearly every event with President and Mrs. Bush, there was a photo opportunity. Guests queue up and give their names to a Marine, who then announces them to the president and first lady. As we moved into our places for the picture, Kay said, "Merry Christmas, Laura," and Mrs. Bush responded, "Merry Christmas, Kay." He almost fell over when he realized he had called the First Lady by her first name. He talked about his faux pas for months afterwards.

The following year at the White House Christmas party, Kay made sure to very properly say, "Merry Christmas, Mrs. Bush."

"It's Laura, Kay," she said, a twinkle in her eye.

And then, a wonderful Christmas present: Later that night, we were following our practice of monitoring the official Senate website and we learned we were confirmed. In one of the last congressional acts before the Senate left town for their holiday recess, a list of presidential appointees was voted on. I made the list. So, after nearly eight months of filling out paperwork, meeting with various entities engaged in the confirmation process, preparing and pondering, observing and being observed, we were more than ready for our Caribbean adventure to begin.

CHAPTER TWO

FROM THE PRAIRIE TO THE MARBLED HALLS

WOW! I really was a U.S. ambassador. People stood when I came into a room...well not in Iowa so much. Information and invitations began pouring in from Washington, from our various countries, and from friends at home who wanted to get together "before we left." I was now addressed as Her Excellency (H.E.). You'd think we were never coming home.

It was a really fun Christmas season. Our friends and family shared our excitement at all the social occasions over the holidays—never any trouble in making conversation. The question "How did you get this job?" was asked over and over again. And my answer "I have no idea why I was chosen!" is still the true answer today. I really do not have a clue how I came to be so blessed, to be given the honor with such a public service opportunity.

Now that I was confirmed and was a "real" ambassador, to do lists exploded. They all required urgent attention. What's the timeline for my resignation from the Iowa Senate? What will we take with us and what is the timing of our travel? Who will get plane tickets and keep everyone in Washington and Barbados informed? Talk about life changes. Before anything else could be done, two critical questions had to be answered. My constituents deserved continuing, hopefully uninterrupted representation, so a special election must be held. Who would run for my Senate seat? And who would replace me as Senate President? Fortunately, Pat Ward, who was serving as the Chief of the Republican Senate Caucus staff, lived in my district and was interested in running. First problem solved; she made a great candidate. Then in late December the caucus met, and our colleagues elected Senator Jeff Lamberti as Senate President. Cool-headed and highly disciplined, he would make good use of the gavel.

Jeff preferred not to preside over the highly protocol-driven opening ceremonies, especially the "State of the State" address, so I agreed to begin the session and preside over the governor's speech one last time. I would then submit my resignation to the governor so the special election could be called. I hoped my constituents would only be without representation for a few weeks. That worked...

Opening day of the Legislative Session began at 7 a.m. with the annual Republican Breakfast. After making my traditional remarks, including a farewell to the group, I received a lengthy standing ovation and was presented with a beautiful crystal clock as a farewell gift. I was surprised to find myself a little weepy. *This leave-taking may be harder than I thought.*

At the Capitol later that morning, my final pre-session media conference with other legislative leaders took place. Our media friends were interested in "How did you get this gig and could we come along—just to carry your suitcase?" Then it was time, 10 a.m. sharp, to bring the gavel down and deliver my opening remarks to my legislative colleagues. The emotional reality began to sink in. I was actually leaving the next day. I confess a tear escaped now and then.

Next day at his "State of the State" address, Governor Tom Vilsack made very gracious and complimentary remarks about my service to the state, and once again I received a prolonged standing ovation. A very touching moment for me and all the family members there. It was truly special to be in the Chamber with our son Kent present as an elected representative. We had been told we were the only mother-son duo serving together (maybe ever—but no one actually researched that) in any legislative body in the country, so our relationship brought an extra poignancy to that historic moment.

And so on January 14, 2004, standing at the podium for the last time in that beautiful Senate Chamber, I swore in Senator Lamberti, congratulated him on his office and his parking space, wished him well, and submitted my official resignation, ending thirteen years of service to the people of Iowa. I was leaving many friends and colleagues and the beautiful office in the State Capitol for the last time. The hardest goodbye of all was to my teammates and office leaders, Becky Beach and Kaye Lozier. The three of us made an effective and efficient team. One of the young high school women who served as a Senate page said it best. She said, "You guys prove it. Chicks rule!" I just loved being a "chick," if only for a moment.

No time to prolong the sadness of leave-taking. Kay and I flew back to Washington that afternoon, to prepare for our swearing-in ceremony. When we arrived at the State Plaza Hotel, our home away from home for the past eight months, we were surprised and delighted to be greeted by a gang of family and friends who had come for the ceremony and to help celebrate.

After numerous champagne toasts, several taxis were summoned and a somewhat rowdy group was off to the Daily Grill for a casual dinner. Secretary of Health and Human Services and former Governor of Wisconsin Tommy Thompson, whom we had seen many times on various campaign trails, recognized us and stopped by the table to offer congratulations.

January 16, 2004, dawned bright, sunny and *cold* in the nation's capital. The Washington reporter for a Des Moines TV station had arranged to interview me outside the State Department that morning. I wore my full-length, fur-lined coat and I was still freezing. She seemed to be colder than I was so it was a very brief interview, but it made the six o'clock news back in Iowa.

After assuring ourselves that everyone had made it through security at the State Department, it was time to move on to my swearing-in. The gathering room outside the Secretary of State's office and the formal Franklin Room where the ceremony took place are beautifully restored—fitting places for serious occasions. During the ceremony, Secretary of State Colin Powell spoke glowingly about my experience and suitability for the posting, then turned to me and asked, "Mary, do you understand your mission?"

"Yes, sir," I said.

"Will you support your troops?"

"Yes, sir, I will."

He turned to the audience with a big smile, and said, "Then you're on my team, sister!"

The room erupted in cheers.

Then it was my turn. Thankfully, my remarks were brief and I managed to deliver them with no major gaffes. The Secretary approached me for the "diplomatic" kiss—an airbrush of both cheeks. I was not accustomed to that second cheek brush and we accidentally rubbed noses. A major gaffe!

"Just a minute, Mary," Secretary Powell said. "Let me show you how to do this."

The audience roared with laughter. They kept laughing as Secretary Powell and I made a second attempt and got it right.

Secretary Powell then escorted me to a historic desk where we signed the documents naming me ambassador. It was official. I was a United States ambassador, the president's personal representative to Barbados and the six other nations of the Eastern Caribbean and the Chief of Mission (COM) of the Embassy in Bridgetown, Barbados.

Afterward, champagne flowed and, with the addition of old friends who lived and worked in Washington and new friends and acquaintances in the State Department and other agencies, more than 300 people joined in the toast to my new career. It seemed as if everyone there had a camera. Kind of like getting married—everyone wants a picture. That evening, a group of friends, family, and colleagues adjourned to the Old Ebbitt's Grill to continue the celebration.

One just cannot have too many parties.

We returned to Iowa one final time to pack and prepare for our move. Since only a few family members and friends could make the trip to Washington for the swearing-in ceremony, we held a second ceremony at the Iowa Capitol in the Senate Chamber. It was full of people—standing room only. Kay held the Bible while newly appointed U.S. District Judge Steve Colloton performed the ceremony. We've known Steve and his family since he and Kent were grade-school classmates in Iowa City. In one of my earlier "lives," I taught music to both Kent and Steve, so it was especially meaningful to have him administer the oath of office.

At the close of the ceremony, our daughter-in-law, Kim, sang "God Bless America." Unaccompanied, she stood on the floor of the Senate and sang from her heart. There wasn't a dry eye anywhere, especially for Kay and me. We stood there holding hands, looking out over the crowd of friends and family, understanding this was truly farewell. We were standing on the bridge to the new adventure.

At 4 a.m. the morning we were to depart for the Caribbean, we awoke to blowing snow and a wind chill of four below zero. Friends Dick and Mary Ann Rosonke arrived at 5 a.m. to drive us to the airport. Only *very* good friends volunteer to be chauffeurs at that hour and temperature.

The Des Moines airport was all abuzz when we arrived that morning. The presence of television cameras and press people got everyone's attention. Through the many months of travel to Washington, the American Airlines people had become our great friends. They greeted us warmly, knowing we were finally continuing on to Miami and then Barbados. The other travelers were fascinated. We actually knew almost everyone in the waiting area, so it was a noisy and talkative group. Finally, we boarded the plane and it was wheels up.

We arrived in Miami, checked into our hotel, ordered soup from room service and crashed. Next morning we took the hotel shuttle to the airport, noted the long lines at check-in and began the wait. It's astounding what people try to take with them on flights to the Caribbean. For starters, four huge shrink-wrapped truck tires. An ATM machine near the ticket counter rapidly spit out cash. People paid hundreds of dollars for overweight baggage charges.

The flight to Bridgetown was wonderful: a welcome relief from all the chaos. We had first-class seats (only offered on the first trip to and the last trip out of an assignment) and the flight crew gave us the royal treatment. We began to have a new appreciation for the respect and attention ambassadors receive. The flight attendants announced we were on board and we received applause from the other passengers. *This is going to be great!*

It was eighty-five degrees and a cloudless blue sky when we touched down in Bridgetown. We were thrilled to see Marcia Bernicat's face in the Embassy group that had come to the airport to greet us. She was the only person we knew in all of the Caribbean. After deplaning, we met numerous members of the Embassy staff in the VIP lounge, and Marcia then introduced us to our driver, Peter JeanBaptiste. My first impression of Peter was that he was extremely fit, very strong and unflappable, with a quiet, reserved nature that at first did not reveal his deep intellectual curiosity. But as we got to know one another and he became more comfortable with me, he proved to be an astute observer, and when encouraged, displayed a deep understanding of foreign policy, taxation, property ownership, all facets of island life. His curiosity even extended to snow-blowing. "Why would anyone want to do that?" he wondered. He became a knowledgeable and trusted advisor on all things Barbados. There was certainly ample opportunity for conversation as he and I spent a lot of time stopped in traffic. The roads in Barbados are simply not built for the number of cars now in use. We had our first experience with some of that traffic that afternoon as Peter drove us from the airport to the residence in the ambassador's vehicle, an armored BMW sedan.

En route Kay and I frantically reviewed names and titles so we'd have some notion of who was who. Every one a new face. The entire country team would be waiting at the residence for a brief meet-and-greet. But looking out over the fields of sugar cane, we realized they were not dissimilar from the corn fields of Iowa—not as large, but green and beautiful.

The first people we met on arrival were the residence staff. Mrs. Rita Bowen, the house manager, introduced us to housekeeper and laundress Norma Richards and butler Ricardo Stay. Then we met the members of the Embassy country team. The country team is comprised of the agency heads of all the major organizations I'd be working with. i.e., the Drug Enforcement Agency (DEA), the Federal Bureau of Investigation (FBI), the Internal Revenue Service (IRS), the Military Liaison Office (MLO), the U.S. Agency for International Development (USAID. the Office of U.S. Foreign Disaster Assistance (OFDA), the Marine Gunnery Sergeant (MSG), and the various leaders of areas of the Department of State, the Consul General (CG) of Barbados, the political/economic officer (pol/econ), the labor officer, the public affairs officer (PAO), the regional security officers (RSO) and so on and so on. These acronyms were only a small sample of Department of State "speak."

Before he left the residence, the RSO demonstrated all the security we would need to engage before we went to bed that night. Then Mrs. Bowen, (not ready to call her Rita just yet) gave us a tour of the residence, known by yet another acronym: CMR, or Chief of Mission Residence. The "CMR" was a beautiful pink stucco home surrounded by palms and beautifully groomed gardens, not only lovely but spotlessly clean. It was apparent that the staff took great pride in their work. We interrupted our tour to gaze out the rear windows to enjoy the beauty of our first Caribbean sunset. It simply stopped us in our tracks. During our years in Barbados, we never became accustomed to, or took that beauty for granted, that was a daily blessing.

After our tour was complete, we began to unpack, being sure we found our toothbrushes and pajamas, when Ricardo appeared in the hallway and cleared his throat. "Dinner is served, Madam Ambassador." Kay and I were ushered to the dining room, where we were seated at a huge table, beautifully set for two with white linen, china, crystal, sterling silver, and candlelight. At its smallest, the table easily sat twelve, so there were ten extra chairs with us that night. The chef's position was open, but somehow Rita and Ricardo still managed to prepare and serve us a formal four-course meal with wine pairings.

It was our first experience with our own personal butler. Ricardo was proficient and charming, and Kay and I couldn't help giggling as he bustled to and from the kitchen. Two amateurs from Iowa getting the royal treatment. We held hands just to make sure we were both awake, not dreaming. *Would every night be like this?*

When it was time for bed, we followed the security procedures we'd been shown. We locked ourselves in the master bedroom and turned on all the alarm systems. There were two large sliding bars on the bedroom door which we engaged. The windows were covered with grillwork. Two telephone systems and a hand-held radio stood at the ready in case of natural disaster or attack. Our bedroom felt like a fortress—or a prison. And Kay asked again: "What have you gotten us into?"

What, indeed, had I gotten us into? My on-the-job training would start in the morning.

When people in Iowa first learned of my nomination, I heard comments like "Wow, nice job if you can get it," or "Gee, how do I get that gig?" I hear similar comments even now, and even after retirement from my three years at Post, and they still make me bristle. Though of course I maintain my endlessly pleasant persona and smile politely. I am from Iowa, after all. Still I feel compelled to say "I worked very hard." Such statements, while good-natured, betray an ignorance of the enormously complex job of the ambassador and the crucial role they play in maintaining and advancing the cause of stable democracies throughout the world. Not me personally—the position is critical to the success of our foreign policy.

That lack of understanding of the role of the ambassador no longer surprises me. I now know the job of ambassador is one of the least understood positions in government. At best, most Americans have only the vaguest notion that ambassadors are "involved in diplomacy," or at worst, they assume that ambassadors are little more than international socialites who cut ribbons and attend cocktail parties, especially if they're political appointees. I confess that at the beginning of my nomination process that was pretty much my impression as well. In reality, ambassadors—even in a veritable paradise like Barbados, with its democratic government and stable economy—face a remarkably complex job. To succeed, one must have a comprehensive knowledge of not only our own country's economic, political, cultural, and social issues but those of the countries we serve in as well. Add to that a need for superior negotiating skills; the ability to function in situations that require extreme multi-tasking; and the temperament to remain coolheaded, logical, yes, "endlessly pleasant" even under verbal fire from elected officials. Alas, the Charm School curriculum didn't even come close to preparing me for the job that awaited me. Not to mention managing 150 employees in four different locations.

In general terms, the job of any American ambassador is to represent the President of the United States abroad. And as I was to quickly learn, I was quite literally the representative of my country. Always "on stage." And that meant any position I took was accepted as the *American* position; any opinion I expressed was assumed to be the opinion of the *American* people. No matter whether I was having a conversation at dinner or at a cocktail reception, speaking at a formal gathering, or simply attending a one-on-one meeting, I was in a fishbowl, on the public stage, and I never forgot it. For example, on a Saturday morning, Kay and I visited the Price Mart, kind of the Costco of Barbados. We were shopping for a new printer for the residence. Our printer did not weather the move very well. A locally employed staff member from the embassy who worked in our warehouse came up to me and said "I wouldn't believe the American ambassador would push her own trolley at the Price Mart if I hadn't seen it for myself." *Oops.* Was this not according to protocol? Certainly we had no security with us—Kay had driven us there in his car. It was a huge responsibility to be the mind and mouth of the United States, and it required *constant vigilance* and a great deal of media savvy. Never a spontaneous moment.

More specifically, my charge from the president was to maintain stable democracies. This was my mission statement, my overall responsibility, and it came directly from President Bush. All seven countries were already democracies, having inherited the parliamentary system from Britain, their former colonial ruler. I was intent on fulfilling my mission to the highest degree possible, and I expected Embassy employees to do the same. But I maintained no illusions about where ultimate responsibility lay. The buck stopped at my desk, or my phone, or my email. Issues that were of critical importance to the seven countries under my charge fell to me, and if I didn't accomplish the mission it was not going to be accomplished. I had been in leadership positions for years, but as an ambassador I felt the pressure to succeed much more keenly than in any previous position. I truly felt responsible for money laundering interruption, for accurately reporting anti-terrorist activities, for slowing the flow of drugs and drug money, for negotiating smooth relations between the countries of the Eastern Caribbean and the rest of the world (especially the U.S.), and for promoting economic development in the Caribbean.

President Bush was right. This job was no walk on the beach.

CHAPTER THREE

ON THE JOB AT LAST

On my first official day, Peter arrived at 8:30 a.m. sharp. The car was immaculate. Of course it was. I learned Peter washed it every morning before meeting me at the front door. It was just a few miles from the residence to the embassy, but it almost always took 45 minutes to an hour to get there through the heavy traffic.

The trip followed the coast road and the beauty of the country, gorgeous vegetation, white sand beaches and the many luxury hotels and villas made every trip interesting.

At the embassy, I dutifully locked my cell phone and my PDA in the lockbox and turned to greet the Marines. The Marines on duty snapped to attention and saluted me. I had been told this would happen every day and I thought I was prepared for it. So I returned the salute—*but with my left hand.* Nothing happened. Nobody moved until Kay nudged me, and I realized my mistake. The Marines, ever professional, simply held their salute until I got it right. I smiled as I saluted properly. To their credit, none of them laughed out loud. At least not while I was in hearing distance. Kay, of course, roared with laughter all the way down the hall to my office.

I spent my first day touring all four locations of the embassy—Embassy Bridgetown itself, the nearby administrative building, the consulate and a warehouse located some distance away. I wanted to meet my new staff immediately, all 150 of them. I shook hands with every employee. They were warm and welcoming, and I looked forward to getting to know them better.

After the hilarity of my incompetent salute, the embassy buildings themselves delivered a nasty shock. They were in execrable condition.

Bird droppings covered the air conditioners, bringing who-knows-what into the air ducts. I learned that several people had already had to shorten their tours of duty and return to the States due to respiratory illness. Vagrants slept on the front steps. Carpets were stained to the point that cleaning them was no longer effective, and the walls had not been painted for years. The elevator had a mind of its own—singing a peculiar song when it was working and requiring a walk up of four flights for employees and their guests when it wasn't. The consulate offices, located in a separate building, had very close neighbors. Some of them were cows that were tethered in grass tall enough to hide them. The building next door was so close, with an outdoor stairway, so that a person could just drop in through the windows of the consul general's office. Across the street from the Embassy the administrative building's main entrance opened onto an alley. So in spite of the regional security officers' best efforts, providing any kind of security standard for our employees was virtually impossible. Even basics like proper lighting and ventilation were problematic. The embassy sat squarely on a busy corner in the middle of bustling Bridgetown. I was first dumbfounded, then livid, that our employees were expected to be productive under these conditions. When I inquired, I was told that due to the imminent opening of the new embassy (then under construction) funds were just not available to mitigate these situations. And besides, they were just temporary. *Right...after I visited the new embassy construction site, I knew there was nothing imminent about an opening.*

I knew about the new embassy being built, as I had met with the Office of Overseas Building Operations (OBO) in Washington—the DOS office responsible for all U.S. government real estate overseas. as part of my orientation. From my visits to OBO, I understood that we would soon be able to move into brand new facilities. Little did I know that the new embassy construction (NEC) project would be a problem that I would struggle to resolve throughout my three years at Post. Looking back, it was no doubt good for my blood pressure levels that I didn't know.

Later in the day, we took a break from the meeting and greeting and had lunch with Office Management Specialist (OMS), Bonita Estes. The OMS is the ambassador's secretary, assistant and confidante. A powerful position. Besides managing all the classified communications and correspondence, Bonita was the lioness at my door. She was an experienced Foreign Service specialist with short red hair, and perpetually outfitted in colors as bright as the island's flora, she prioritized all the communications and meeting requests for my attention, determined who should have time on the ambassadorial calendar. She also sorted through the multiple invitations and meeting requests I received daily, advising me on which ones were "command performances" and which ones were just "maybes." She was very protective of my time and the insisted on correct protocol for all interactions with me. Thankfully, she also managed the all-important expense reports and worked with house manager Rita Bowen to prepare the residence expense reports. Bonita served at several embassies, and she was posted in Nairobi when that embassy was bombed in 1998. Seasoned and knowledgeable, she had a great sense of humor and shared my expectation that we could have fun at work. She knew her way around the embassy, the people, the processes and the island, and she made work enjoyable. At lunch that day she gave me a crash course in "must know," "must see," and "must do" on Barbados. Her schooling was so comprehensive we learned which restaurants were "fun" and which were "elegant," that Cool Runnings was the best catamaran cruise and that Bubba's, a local sports bar, would carry Iowa Hawkeye games on television, much to Kay's delight.

Later that afternoon, Peter drove us to the Holetown police station to apply for our Barbados driver's licenses—one of the necessities of living on Barbados. Holetown is a small, colorful, historic community near the residence. Much of the retail business operated in small "chattel" houses, each one a separate business. Scattered about between them were tables where entrepreneurs sold jewelry and coconut water, and enterprising women braided hair. On the corner across the street from the police station was the island supermarket, "The Super Centre." The station itself was a noisy, rowdy place located right on the white sands of the beach by the glittering blue water. Just before we arrived, a school bus had stopped at the station to seek help. It seemed that some children on board had seriously misbehaved. The driver just drove straight to the police station and parked the bus in the middle of the parking lot. The children were escorted into the station. The young officer taking our application didn't bat an eye as his fellow police officers escorted loud and angry children to a room just past us. I have no idea what the misbehavior was, or how the police handled that afternoon's delinquents, and I didn't ask. The unflappable officer recorded our information in a large book in pencil. He asked why we had moved to Barbados. When I told him what my position was he put his pencil down, straightened up, looked me in the eye and said, "You are the new U.S. ambassador?"

I smiled and nodded.

"Can you get me a visa to go to the U.S.?"

Visas were so much in demand throughout all seven of my countries; I came to wish that I had a dollar for every time someone asked me that.

After our temporary driver's licenses were issued, Peter drove us back to the residence. The cool quiet was welcome after a long day. We passed right on through to the bedroom to change clothes; no matter how we thought we had adjusted our business wardrobe for the tropics, we were still hot.

Then we discovered that all of our clothing had been washed, pressed, folded, and neatly stacked on our bed. Everything looked new. Even our t-shirts were pressed. Norma was a godsend, and we had a new appreciation of the kind of service that was going to be a part of our lives.

Next day was our first Saturday, and Kay and I were taken on a "windshield tour" of Barbados. We travelled in an embassy van with Peter behind the wheel and Administrative Officer Leo Voytko acting as navigator. John Regan, a junior Foreign Service officer in the U.S. Consulate who had been assigned to look after us, and Juanita, a locally employed staff member of the Public Diplomacy Office, with a marvelous lilting Bajan accent, were also along for the ride and acted as both guides and storytellers. John, full of energy and enthusiasm in his horn-rimmed glasses and blue buttoned down shirt, was a remarkably attentive person who was eerily good at anticipating my needs and my questions. As such, he insisted we make our first stop at Flindts' for coffee and pastries. Good call. They were wonderful. It seems he understood me very well already. He had a wonderfully quick wit and was well known and well liked throughout the island. Juanita relished her role relating local legend and folklore as well as practical economic and business information. She clearly took pride in her country and enjoyed sharing her wealth of knowledge with us.

I found myself so entranced with the beauty of the island; I listened to John and Juanita with half an ear. The pictures in adventure guides and travel brochures don't begin to do justice to the Barbados countryside. America has special beauty "from sea to shining sea," but Barbados is a small, never-ending tropical paradise. From the pictures, I expected the white sandy beaches and clear, turquoise waters. But coming from a wintry landscape, I was taken aback by the sheer profusion of color. The aptly named Pride of Barbados, a golden flowering shrub that blooms year-round, was everywhere, the bougainvillea were blooming profusely in every shade of pink, purple orange, and red, just growing wild on the island. The huge flamboyant trees were in fiery bloom, simply covered with huge red blossoms. In the public parks and in private gardens, it was common to see hibiscus trees, (yes trees, not bushes) birds of paradise, anthuriums in every imaginable color, orchids of every size and variety—all exotic plants that struck my eye. We drove through historic mahogany forests, and passed amazingly well preserved seventeenth century plantation houses, still occupied. Even the general vegetation, including the spiky leaves of the thousands of palm trees dotting the island, received our attention: They were a shade of deep emerald green only found in a tropical climate. The acres of sugar cane fields, however, made us feel at home. They were a miniature version of the rolling corn fields in Iowa, except there were no fences and they grew right up to the edge of the road.

Barbados is an island formed on coral formations with very visible large outcroppings of rock. Some places those outcroppings were cliffs with "gullies" between them. These differences in elevation were particularly apparent in relation to the seas. Bridgetown, which is located on the southwest side of the island on the Caribbean, enjoys serene waters and broad white sandy beaches, with shades of turquoise blue growing shades darker as the water deepens. But at the northernmost point of the island (known sensibly enough as North Point), the mingling Caribbean Sea and the Atlantic Ocean crashed onto high, craggy rock formations. There was no landmass between there and the coast of Africa 3,000 miles away. The Atlantic side of Barbados reminded me of a much warmer version of the often stormy Pacific Ocean off the coast of Oregon in the U.S. We traveled down the eastern shore of the island, where the Atlantic tides and surf were home to some of the greatest surfboarding terrain in the world. "Second only to the Fiji islands as the best surfing location in the world," Juanita told us. And sure enough, we saw surfers seemingly taking their lives in their hands with every wave. Finally we curved around the South Beach and again met with the gorgeous turquoise waters and the white sands. And one resort hotel after another. Picture Miami Beach in miniature, with hotels in lovely pastel colors, no more than four or five stories tall. We learned that St. Lawrence Gap, or The Gap as it's commonly known, was "the happenin' place" on the island. It was the gathering place for young travelers, those in search of steel pan calypso music, fish markets, bars that served the island's famous Banks Beer, and the ultimate t-shirt and souvenir shops. Apparently it came to life around 10 p.m. each night. Later, the Regional Security Officer suggested that it was not a place we should plan to frequent at night. No problem. We weren't in the habit of frequenting *any* place late at night.

We stopped for lunch at the Round House, a historic bed and breakfast perched high above the Atlantic on Barbados' east coast. The view from the open windows there was picture-postcard perfect. We were encouraged to try the flying fish sandwich with breadfruit fries for lunch. Flying fish is the national dish of the island, and breadfruit trees produce their starchy fruits in abundance. We found both delicious. Kay normally doesn't enjoy fish but was a good sport and went for it. Even he enjoyed his lunch. Our waitress shyly asked if we would come to the kitchen so the staff could greet the new ambassador. Of course. In the kitchen I shook everyone's hand and thanked them for a delicious meal. "You are most welcome, Madam Ambassador," a very large cook in a smeared white apron said. "Can you please get us visas to go to the U.S.?" From the row of smiling, expectant faces, I could see that he spoke on behalf of the entire staff. People in the Caribbean truly believe that America is the land of opportunity. It was humbling to encounter such unabashed faith in the American dream, especially as so many of our own citizens seem to feel only entitlement and take the opportunities for granted. Immigrants from the Eastern Caribbean are known in America as hard working and successful people.

Many employers in the U.S., particularly in the tourism industry, deliberately seek Caribbean employees. Nearly everyone in these islands has relatives in the U.S.

This drive around the island was pure pleasure. We became better acquainted with the island and with the key members of staff, and learned some important survival lessons that would serve us well. We drove down the "wrong" side of the road (part of Barbados' British heritage). There were few stop signs or stop lights; instead there were many roundabouts. The roads and streets in Barbados (and the potholed paths we were on at times could only charitably be called roads) have no names or signs. Oh, there are wooden signs on posts from time to time pointing the way to some attraction or other—actually they pointed to Paris, Rome, Miami, and Africa, as well as the Children's Garden, Gordon's Cave and Earthworks Pottery. So, the best way to navigate, at least until one gets the lay of the land, is to understand the bus signs. There are two phrases: "to the city" and "away from the city." Which city? Bridgetown. A little vague perhaps, but this knowledge became extremely useful several weeks later when Kay and I, along with friends who'd come to visit, decided to explore the east side of the island and got ourselves lost. We ended up at a lighthouse that had a sign that said it was the last stop before Africa, which we absolutely believed to be true. But with the "to the city" and "away from the city" signs, along with the help of the friendly vicar of Codrington College, we got directions back to Holetown and made it home.

We ended our first Saturday tour by driving through Bridgetown before being dropped at the residence. We realized we'd completely circled the island in six hours. Our love affair with a beautiful land and a beautiful people had begun.

The official schedule had us jumping right in to the deep end of the social whirl. After the windshield tour we barely had time to get dressed before Peter returned to drive us to Marcia Bernicat's for dinner with the country team and their spouses and significant others—more than forty people. We needed to get acquainted immediately. Marcia's residence provided our first experience with alfresco dining. The only windows with glass in them in the house were in the bedrooms, the bathrooms and the formal dining room. Everything else was open so the residents could enjoy the views and the wonderful island breezes. After sunset, however, the breeze often stops, making evenings the warmest time of the day.

At Marcia's I heard a story that taught an important lesson about the alfresco life: Food cannot be left unattended because monkeys will come in and eat it. At first I thought my sense of humor was being tested—but that was for real. Marcia told the story of an American Woman's Club meeting held at her residence. The guests all brought desserts and left them on tables upstairs. They went down to the first floor for their meeting, and when they came up to enjoy their refreshments, there were monkeys everywhere and every dish had been devoured.

The Legal Attaché, representing the FBI, took Kay under her wing and taught him another valuable Barbados lesson. "Always sit first," she said. "That way you get the seat closest to the window and directly under the fan." Later Kay said he would sit next to Susan any time, nevermind the fan or the window—she was blond and beautiful.

The next day was Super Bowl Sunday, and the Marines were hosting a game-watch party at the Marine House, the living quarters for the seven members of the U.S. Marine detachment on the island. The Marines are assigned the duty of protecting the property and the classified information at every embassy throughout the world. They are an outstanding group of young people, most of them 19 and 20 year olds, who are prepared to give their lives to protect the Embassy, its people and their country. The group gathered included many of the Americans on the island and their families. The hospitality at Marine Houses is legendary and a worldwide tradition. We were invited, it was important to get to know our colleagues quickly, so we went. Clearly our attendance was unexpected. A group of very at ease Marines in shorts and t-shirts scrambled to stand and salute and be of service in any way possible. Even the children seemed to understand protocol. They were immediately on their best behavior and addressed me as "Madam Ambassador." Obviously, we were considered the grown-ups, and we really put a chill on that party. Around me, the Marines were consummate professionals at all times, and solicitous hosts. Kay and I only stayed a short while, "worked the room," greeted everyone there and left—so the good times could resume. Peter was waiting at the door to take us home. We spent the rest of the day getting unpacked and trying to feel settled in our new home.

On Monday, after a busy day of paper work at the office, we were entertained at dinner by the British High Commissioner and his wife at their residence, which boasted absolutely fabulous gardens. As in most homes on Barbados, the living areas were not air conditioned. In fact, most Barbadians do not like air conditioning. That evening, we dined alfresco on their huge verandah overlooking the gardens. This five-course meal with wine pairings rivaled our first night at the residence with Ricardo. We again found ourselves overfed and overly warm in the tropical heat. Definitely we were not yet acclimated, and our wardrobes, appropriate for summer in Iowa, were definitely not "cool" enough. After dinner, we adjourned to another seating area on their verandah for after dinner drinks. H.C. White insisted we try the very smooth Mount Gay Reserve Rum, a Barbadian specialty. It was smooth and delightful sipping. However, after about two sips, I realized I was in danger of falling asleep and sliding off my chair onto the floor. Certainly not good form for the new U.S. ambassador. Fortunately Kay was feeling much as I was: he spied my drooping eyelids and had the presence of mind to stand and begin our farewells.

Moments later I got my first inkling that Peter had some sort of sixth sense. I don't believe he could see where we were sitting from where he was parked, but miraculously the car appeared at the front door just as we did. He managed to repeat this feat many times over my three years on island, which never ceased to amaze me. Later, I wondered if the man had slipped a chip into my head that chimed when I stood to leave.

Two nights later we enjoyed our next big social engagement. Business leader Sir Alan Fields and his wife Lady Irene entertained Kay and me, Marcia, and Chief Political Officer Paul Belmont at dinner at The Tides, a world-class restaurant on the west coast of the island. Sir Alan was a senator, appointed by the prime minister, and an officer at BS&T (Barbados Shipping and Trading Company). This company included subsidiaries as diverse as the BMW dealership, the Super Centre Grocery Stores, and Banks Beer Brewery, among others. We enjoyed the evening on the beach at a large octagonal table under a fan. Included on the guest list were two other couples who were leaders in the Barbados business community. Sir Charles Williams (Sir Charles, who was called Carl, and was an expert polo player as well as having a construction and development company), his wife Lady Mary Ann who raised horses, and Paul Altman (Paul's companies dealt in commercial and residential real estate sales and development), and his wife Rachelle, an artist. These three couples were knowledgeable and influential leaders in Barbadian society. I asked them to share the issues and concerns they felt were important for me to know. The lively conversation ranged from the local economy to the popularity of the current government, to cricket, polo, and the social scene. I shared my charge of maintaining stable democracies and my belief that democracies cannot remain stable without a growing, job-creating economy. That message was music to the ears of this group.

That evening we began to understand how business gets done on the island. With all the socializing on my calendar, I had already started to become a tad worried that I might become a decorative ribbon cutter, flitting from one social event to another without accomplishing much. In fact, it became clear almost immediately that much could be accomplished, relationships built and agendas moved forward at social occasions; very similar to the political world in the U.S. More often than not, it is within the context of a social gathering that business gets accomplished in the Caribbean. We were in the laidback island culture and operating on island time, "no worries, mon," and I needed to function within that system. Community and business leaders, locals especially, thought nothing of having an hour of conversation over rum punches and then getting into serious issues. Iowa isn't known for its fast pace or rum punches, and I still had a bit of a struggle adjusting to island time.

As it turned out, that evening at The Tides, as fun as it was, proved to be enormously beneficial. These couples became great friends to us, and they were extremely helpful throughout our time in the islands in giving advice, providing insight into the business community, and including us in social events, where we were able to enlarge our circle of friends and colleagues. These folks knew who had information, who had the ear of various government leaders, and what we could do to more fully participate in the society of the country. It was largely because of them that I was able to rapidly gain knowledge about the economics of Barbados, things I needed to know as I worked on our trade and job creation goals.

Prior to our arrival, Marcia asked John Regan to prepare three three-ring binders for us. They proved to be an invaluable resource. The first contained information about everything one could possibly want to know about Barbados—demographics, politics, business, religion, culture, maps, even some local slang. (I'd already learned two important slang words: "liming," which describes the island-wide habit of just hanging out, and "Bajan," which is how the locals refer to themselves.) The second binder had a picture and brief biography of every embassy employee. The third included a tentative schedule for my first six weeks at Post. A schedule that established the time lines necessary for achieving my goal of completing credential presentation. I would not be able to conduct any official business until credentials were presented, so my bias for action took over. On Tuesday of that first week on the job, an all-employee meeting was scheduled. My goal was to introduce Kay and me more fully by sharing how much we were anticipating enjoying the beautiful island and making new friends, as well as some things about my leadership style and expectations. For example, I wanted them to know *I never shoot messengers.* After sharing my audacious goal of presenting credentials on every island in six weeks, I could see that the somewhat laidback staff was astonished—and doubtful. As I told them, "Our schedule does not allow any time for "'liming'." That remark was met with laughter and applause.

The largest part of my hours in the office that first week was spent completing more paperwork. I had to certify a complete inventory of the residence, renew the contracts for the residence staff, and prepare expense reports to recover the costs of our travel to Post. The residence inventory had to be completed, including counting silverware and kitchen tools, bed linens and towels. How wonderful for me—Administrative Officer Leo Voytko and Mrs. Bowen had been through this before, so it was accomplished with great dispatch. Meanwhile, I was at work in Barbados and I still didn't know what I would be paid or what benefits I was to have. Apparently there is a website with all this information on it, but it required classified passwords to log on, and I had no idea how to get them. Bonita to the rescue.

The Barbados immigration department also required lots of paperwork, which meant more multi-copy forms to complete and briefings to attend. We learned it was a good thing we did not intend for Kay to seek employment. The government of Barbados is not hospitable to family members of embassy personnel who want to get jobs. Work permits are nearly impossible to get. This struck me as a completely incongruous stance, since there was already a constant stream of personal requests for visa assistance to allow Bajans to go the U.S. and work. These small nations expect that the hundreds of Caribbean folks who get visas will be able to find employment immediately when they reach the U.S., but they refuse to reciprocate with the few Americans who accompany their spouses as they serve in Barbados. This becomes even more difficult to under-stand when one realizes that remittances—the money those Caribbean workers in the U.S. send back to their families—make up a huge percentage of foreign revenue; on some islands more than fifty percent.

I presided over my first country team meeting and core team meeting. The smaller core team, a sub-set of the country team, involved only the law-enforcement heads, and was a classified meeting held in a secure space in the embassy. After those meetings, it was apparent what my first manage-ment task would be. We had some serious teamwork issues that needed to be addressed pronto if we were to have any hope of getting meaningful work accomplished. It seemed that no one considered themselves a member of a "team." Instead, everyone wanted to pursue their own individual missions, not seeing the larger picture of the collective embassy mission—maintaining stable democracies. And of course each agency head thought *their* mission was of primary importance, trumping all others, and each deserving of the ambassador's immediate attention. So before I even mastered logging on to my computer system, I started devising a plan to build my group of single practitioners, the so-called country team, into a real team. I also asked Bonita to begin scheduling meetings with each member of the country team. I pre-ferred to visit with them in their offices, and the agenda included asking them to talk to me about their mission and goals, and share how best I could assist them in accomplishing their goals. Meanwhile, Bonita and I solidified the plans to present credentials to all seven countries within six weeks. This sent the political and economic officers scurrying to prepare briefing materials for me. Finally, not neglecting the importance of the social occasion, plans were made and invitations sent for my welcome reception.

We experienced how it felt to be treated like royalty; and why. Because the ambassador is the representative of the president. People stood when we came into the room. Our house staff was so anxious to please—doing every-thing they could to make us comfortable—sometimes knowing what we needed even before we did ourselves. It was made very clear during our security training that I was never to drive myself—or even to be alone in a car. I had a driver who was my protector and would cheerfully appear at any time of the day or night to drive me where I needed to go, no matter whether the trip was personal or professional. Like most Iowans, we were completely unaccustomed to being served in this way. But you can believe we adjusted immediately and began to enjoy the experience. *It was not difficult.* Having the luxury of someone else taking care of everything, from grocery shopping, knowing where the best fresh fruits and vegetables could be found, doing all the housekeeping and the laundry, even planning menus and preparing meals was remarkable. We were politely scolded for making the bed in the morning. There was no excuse for not accomplishing goals on the job; all other respon-sibilities were well covered.

With all that said however, it was immediately clear that the ambassador was the responsible person. Issues that arrived at my desk came to my phone or my email were of critical importance to my country. Even if I was not well versed on the issue itself, I needed to get the necessary information and respond. I accepted the fact that if I didn't accomplish the mission—it was not going to be accomplished. I felt pressured to achieve goals and handle problems and issues much more keenly than in any of my many and varied past positions. I truly felt responsible for interrupting money laundering, for following and reporting suspected terrorist activities in the region, for issuing visas appropriately and carefully, for slowing the massive trafficking of drugs, money and people, for changing perceptions of my country for the better so that heads of government could understand and even embrace some of the requests for support that we could send their way. Expectations I had for myself were sky high. This truly was "no walk on the beach."

I had been on the job less than one week.

CHAPTER FOUR

FIRST ORDER OF BUSINESS? PRESENT CREDENTIALS

Look out Caribbean! Mary's here and ready to go...but, before I could become a "real" person, speak with government officials, or have our possessions cleared by customs and delivered to the residence, I had to present my credentials to the head of state in each of my countries. Presenting credentials proved to be a somewhat nerve-wracking experience. Kind of like a first piano recital. Each of the islands had a unique, formal, and protocol-driven process. We needed to be prepared for each in great detail—right down to where to stand on the carpet, when we stepped forward and when to shake hands. It was choreographed to the last degree. Each event was purely ceremonial, we were creating a first impression—and you only get one chance at a first impression. The governor general, titular head of each government, must receive my formal letters of appointment from the president. Although unlikely, they could decide they didn't want to accept me, I was comforted to know that if there was a problem with me it would have been signaled to the White House months ago. Still, the possibility existed. Traveling to all seven islands and going through a unique process seven times was a whirlwind of activity. Learning came fast and furious—both personal and professional.

Every island visit revealed more specifics of what my job would entail—we heard about more of the dark underbelly of extreme poverty, crime, corruption, and economic uncertainty behind the sun-drenched images one sees on postcards or travel guides.

But, on to the credentials presentations.

My credentials consisted of the letter of appointment from the president, the formal document recalling the previous ambassador, and the formal documents naming me as ambassador, each affixed with the presidential seal and each in its own large white envelope.

As I described earlier, when Marcia and I met in Washington in December, we agreed I would attempt to present credentials to all seven islands within my first six weeks at Post. It was an audacious goal, and embassy staff was astonished and, as they shared with Marcia, privately doubtful. Although no one argued with me, I could tell some of them were thinking "Sure you can." Meaning, *"Not." I actually began to have doubts myself, but I was not ready to share them with anyone, not even Kay.*

Foreign Service Officer John Regan continued to provide assistance during our first weeks in Barbados. John accepted his role with energy and enthusiasm. He became a good friend and loyal supporter. Marcia and John, along with Bonita and Paul Belmont, the Chief Political Affairs Officer, and his staff members, formed the team that would implement the plan. Scheduling appointments and events on each island would be no small task, especially since government officials might not be interested in meeting with me as quickly as I wanted to meet with them. All the travel expenses for presentations would deplete a huge chunk of our travel budget for the entire year, so we decided that I should not just fly in, drop off my credentials, and fly out. You just can't get in the car and drive to Antigua—or any other island. We tried to schedule as many appointments with government officials and other island leaders as possible, and arrange for several social occasions on each island during our stay. In addition to government officials, we wanted to create opportunities for us to visit with the business community, American expatriates who lived, worked or owned property on the islands, and in some cases, local religious and education leaders as well.

This required lots of work on the part of the political/economic officers as well as the other agency heads at the embassy. They proved themselves up to the task. I just loved the diplomatic term "briefing." Brief would not be the operative word for this activity. Briefings usually consisted of the preparation of white papers providing insight into the government, trade, culture, American involvement, who likes us and who doesn't. Since Kay and I were going together on this round of visits, we were both given the best and most accurate information available about the feelings of the various government officials toward the U.S. We were provided with best guess ideas about issues that might be presented to us during these early meetings and what my proper responses would be. We learned about issues that had recently caused friction or been mutually beneficial so I could speak to those directly. My colleagues were relieved to learn that I preferred to speak in public without reading my remarks.

I preferred talking points, and I expected briefs to be brief; actually verbally delivered using talking points would be most helpful. I could literally see their relief; almost hear the "Whew."

Lists were developed of people who should be invited to our planned social occasions. Since there was no money in the budget for such gatherings, staff was challenged to find sponsors on each island who saw value in our approach and would contribute funds to help allay the costs of each occasion.

To their everlasting credit, this team, with Marcia on point, started working on this in December right after my confirmation vote, so they were prepared to present me with the completed plan during my first week in Barbados. I took a look at the plan, said "Great work. Let's do it." Shock and awe. No changes or alterations. Everyone went to work, got on the phones arranging appointments, party venues, hotel reservations and plane tickets, everything that was needed to execute our plan.

Meantime, we received a call from Hughey Allman, the Acting Chief of Protocol for the Barbados government, saying the governor general was ready to receive me to present credentials. This was unheard of. I had been on island less than a week and we had received the invitation and were scheduled to present credentials in Barbados.

A word about governors general. In the parliamentary form of government, in countries who are a part of the British Commonwealth of Nations, the governor general is nominated by the prime minister and appointed by the Queen. That person then serves as the queen's representative. The prime minister is elected by a vote of the people and serves as the actual operational head of government and as the leader of the majority party of the Parliament as well. The prime minister has the real power in each country.

We met with Hughey the day before the presentation to go over the details. He was thorough and helpful. After receiving the directions, I began praying I could balance all those formal white envelopes and the folder with my prepared remarks while I was fumbling to hand them over. By the way, my formal remarks for credentials presentation had to be written out because they were to be handed over to the governor general and copies provided to the media present.

On the morning of day five on island, the Governor General of Barbados received us to present our credentials. Another beautiful day in paradise—the sun was shining, the sky was cloudless, and it was *hot*. Thirty minutes before our appointment, a member of the governor general's security staff arrived at the embassy to meet Kay and me. She introduced us to the uniformed police-man who would be our driver, and we got in the car provided and proceeded to the residence of the governor general, where the ceremony would take place. The governor's staff person was a young woman in full military dress. In the Caribbean the uniform for women law enforcement officers includes a jacket, skirt, and hat. There is a military style belt with an over the shoulder cross strap, which looked quite uncomfortable over her rather large bosom. She was also equipped with a sidearm and a saber. Unfortunately the saber was a little too long, so it banged on the floor with every step, making it quite difficult for her to walk, open doors, or get in and out of the car. She did not seem to notice anything amiss. Our driver was wearing full dress whites with red and gold braid and epaulets. After the introductions, neither one of them spoke again while we were en route.

When we arrived at Government House, Hughey Allman and the entire media corps of Barbados were on hand to greet us. Our escorts were obviously thrilled to be on television and have their pictures taken. I carried my credentials, those multiple large white envelopes which had been prepared at the White House and sealed with the presidential seal. We were ushered into the foyer and up the stairs to the formal meeting room. Our instructions were reviewed. There was a small rug on the floor and I was to stand at the edge of the rug, facing the governor general. Kay was to stand somewhat behind me and to the right. We were not to step on the rug or offer to shake hands until the credentials had been exchanged.

Governor General Sir Clifford Husbands and Lady Husbands arrived after we were in our places. He handed me the letter of recall for the previous U.S. ambassador and made his formal welcoming remarks. I received those credentials (yet another large white envelope to manage), and handed over my credentials to him. *So far so good, I haven't dropped anything yet.* The governor general made his formal remarks and then he invited me to make my prepared remarks, mostly about how flattered we are to be presented so soon after my arrival, our appreciation for the beauty of the country and the friendliness of the people, and my desire to work together for the betterment of both our countries. *Please God, don't let me drop anything.* Only then could I hand off all the envelopes and the copies of my remarks and step across the rug to shake hands. We each introduced our spouses. Many pictures were taken as the handover and the handshakes were repeated several times for the media. We then adjourned to the "parlor" for a visit. This was a huge, formal residence—in the style of a plantation house. The formal rooms were on the second floor with the large windows wide open to receive all the ocean breezes—at the top of a gorgeous, red carpeted staircase. The room was furnished with beautiful antique pieces of the British Empire style. In the early colonial days this was the residence of the British governor. One wall was dominated with a larger than life full length portrait of Queen Elizabeth II in her younger days; in formal dress, jewels and crown. Queen Elizabeth II is still regarded at the titular monarch of Barbados, and in five of my other six countries. Only Dominica varies from this pattern.

Governor General Sir Clifford Husbands was a charming and gracious host. He spent over an hour with us, serving us juice or water (no ice). It was very clear he wanted us to be at home in his country and he wanted a good relationship with the U.S. He told me he understood the friendship between our two countries was quite strained and he offered to be of assistance as we worked to improve our relationship. Foreign Minister Dame Billie Miller made several very critical speeches in the Parliament over the last months and Washington was not pleased. During those remarks, she also made it clear the length of time without an ambassador was insulting to their country and the region. As a result, the relationship between our countries was a bit chilly. I told him my motto, "Don't look back, we're not going that way," and that I was prepared to do everything I could to improve the working relationship of our two countries. We closed our visit with his promise to attend events when invited and he assured me he would be available to talk at any time.

When we came out to return to the embassy, the American Flag was flying on the front on the car. An emotional moment for me; seeing the flag on that car brought home to me the significance of representing our country. On the return trip, we were escorted by the same two officers. This time they were talkative and personable, absolutely charming. We enjoyed a good visit and it was obvious we were now considered "real" people.

Keeping up with that ambitious schedule, we flew to Grenada in the evening after presenting credentials in Barbados. We scheduled our visit to coincide with their National Days celebration, the equivalent of our Independence Day, 4th of July celebrations. These small islands were all former British colonies, so their independence came as a "gift" from Great Britain. It was not won as a result of a revolution or a coup d'état. Since these were relatively young democracies (25 to 30 years old), their independence was still very fresh, and the celebrations were a great source of national pride, with nearly everyone participating in some way.

During my morning with the Barbados governor general, the Charge d'Affaires of the consulate in Grenada had called Bonita and told her I would be expected to wear a hat for the credential presentation. *What?* I hadn't worn a hat except to keep my head warm for at least thirty years. *There is no hat in my wardrobe! And we fly out in about two hours.*

Peter to the rescue. "Peter," I said, "it's an emergency. Where do I find hats?" Without blinking an eye, he drove me to several stores, came in to each store with me, and shared his expertise on which hats would be "appropriate" for various occasions. Caribbean women often wear hats, so there was a large selection and they were very fashionable and very expensive. With Peter's assistance, I acquired a very businesslike black straw hat. I would be properly costumed for the trip to Grenada. Whew!

As we arrived at the airport, we had our first experience with the Barbados protocol officers escorting us to the airport V.I.P. lounge. Airport employees saluted as we passed by and we were in the lounge in no time. Beautifully decorated, with floral print sofas and chairs; coffee tables covered with magazines and newspapers and large screen televisions at various locations throughout the room. No need to check in or handle our bags, Peter and the protocol staff handled everything. We were offered refreshments when we arrived in the lounge. Coffee, tea, wine, rum, biscuits. Lovely way to travel.

Sharing the VIP lounge with us that evening were St. Vincent and the Grenadines Prime Minister Ralph Gonsolves and his beautiful wife. Even though we had not been formally presented in St. Vincent, Ralph was expansive and friendly. He insisted on being called by his first name and told me to give George (President Bush) his best and thank him for sending such a beautiful and brilliant ambassador this time. Hmmm. A very large Latin man (his ancestors emigrated from Portugal), and given to effusive praise and hand kissing...bluntly put, "he was full of it." Ralph explained he was on his way to New York to meet with Donald Trump. We learned later he sold the Grenadine island of Canouan to Trump, who developed an exclusive five star resort and golf course there. As we departed, Ralph again wanted to be sure I gave his best regards to "GW," explaining how they recently became great friends at a meeting in South America. Hmmm...

Arriving in Grenada, we were met at the airport by the American Charge d'Affaires and a local employee/driver. Grenada was the only island in my group that had an office location and an American staffer. This had been the case since the "American intervention" occurred in the 1980s. We were driven to the Calabash Hotel. All rooms were suites; two suites to each thatched cottage. Our suite was on the second floor. Snacks and wine had been placed in the room; thank goodness, we were starving. We completed our breakfast order so it could be served on our verandah in the morning.

Sure enough, promptly at 7:30 a.m., the servers arrived with white tablecloth, china and silver, and we were served omelets, toast, fresh melon, berries, and papaya. We enjoyed breakfast on our balcony, overlooking a gorgeous white sand crescent of beach. The food service at the Calabash hotel was directed by the renowned British chef, Rhodes. First class. Each set of four cottages had a small separate building in the rear that contains a kitchen, so our breakfast was prepared right downstairs. If we had more time, we could have had lunch and dinner served the same way, or spent time in the restaurant.

We prepared to meet the Grenada governor general by getting into full dress mode. Kay in suit and tie and me in a black suit and my new hat. Still not acclimated, we were both sweltering. As we walked to the car, we passed other hotel guests sitting on their verandahs in their swimsuits, enjoying their breakfast and their newspapers. They waved and greeted us as we passed by. It was *painfully obvious we were not on vacation.*

Again, the credential presentation was very formal and protocol driven. This time our staff drove us to Government House, the formal and historic residence of the governor general. When we arrived, the media present engaged in much picture taking, and then the protocol officers led us inside and explained the ceremony to us. We awaited the arrival of the governor general. First, four beautifully costumed, somewhat senior women arrived and took their places, all wearing elegant hats. Then two uniformed security officers stepped into the room with herald trumpets. The governor general made his entrance, coming down a broad flight of stairs while the herald trumpets attempted to play "Ruffles and Flourishes." Kay and I deliberately kept our eyes straight ahead. To make eye contact would surely have caused an eruption of extremely undiplomatic mirth. *Bite your lip!* We completed the exchange of envelopes; each delivered our formal remarks, completed the "rug dance" and shook hands. The women and the trumpeters left immediately after the exchange of credentials and the formal remarks. We never learned who they were. After the ceremony was completed, and the media had their pictures, we were invited to have juice or tea and a lovely chat.

During tea, I asked the governor general what we could do to improve relations between our two countries. He immediately answered, "Send me more Peace Corps Volunteers, they are America's best diplomatic weapon." Almost two hours of lively conversation followed. Neither his staff nor mine could get him to conclude the interview. The schedule was going to be at least an hour off, but he was obviously enjoying himself!

When we came out, the American flag was mounted on the right front of our car and the State Department Chief of Mission flag on the left. Another moment of great pride and a reminder that we were representing our country in this place. Big lumps in our throats.

A whirlwind of appointments followed. We met with several government ministers including Foreign Minister Nimrod (his real name). Everyone received us graciously, even though we were an hour late.

Later that afternoon, I had a television interview that turned out to be an attempted ambush. Every question was phrased in a contentious manner. Why doesn't America do this or that, ranting on about how terrible we are in Iraq, opining that Grenadians do not respect the U.S. President and complaining bitterly about how the U.S. had ignored Grenada for years. Even though I tried to respond, I was continually interrupted. I remained cool, that endlessly pleasant thing, and managed to make a few points about how we were honored to be in Grenada, how gracious the governor general had been and how we looked forward to working with all Grenadians. I refused to give interviews to that station in ensuing visits. When I visited, we always set up media appearances, and they were simply not invited. After several months of being ignored, the general manager of the station asked the Charge if I would grant an interview if he was the questioner. I accepted, he apologized on camera for the tone of the previous discussion, and we had a good discussion of issues. Point made and problem solved.

We enjoyed a late lunch at a beautiful beachfront restaurant with the members of the diplomatic corps of Grenada, which consisted of ambassadors from Taiwan, Venezuela, and Cuba. Everyone spoke a little English, so we could carry on a conversation, mostly about the weather and the lovely food. I remembered my protocol instructions, which suggested it was fine to be respectful to the Cuban, but do not shake hands and NEVER have one's picture taken with him. *So noted.*

That evening, there was a welcome reception at the home of the American Charge. It was crowded and HOT. A surprisingly number of Americans attended, including faculty members from St. George's University and individuals from the yachting community. St. George's University is a U.S. university with a large medical school. They provided education opportunities to students who could not find space due to the limited enrollments of medical schools in America. The university has about 1,000 American students and faculty members. The 1983 "intervention" occurred largely to protect the students and faculty from the chaos of a revolution. We met many unforgettable characters at this gathering. The "yachties" were unique and diverse, ranging from suntanned couples in shorts and t-shirts who have small boats and a great sense of adventure, to the beautifully dressed people who have huge yachts and crews to pilot them as they travel to locations around the world.

Next morning we were scheduled for a bus tour as part of the government hospitality for members of the visiting diplomatic corps. We were told the dress would be casual. Included in the tour were the local diplomatic corps and a number of non-resident ambassadors who were there for the National Day celebrations. Kay and I were quite casually dressed when word came the prime minister had changed his schedule and would like to meet with us immediately. No time to change so we had our pictures taken with Kay in his Tommy Bahama shirt and me in my short sleeve pantsuit, both of us quite a bit taller than the PM, who stood between us, dressed in his suit and tie.

Contrary to the opinion expressed by the TV reporter, most Grenadians have a great love for the United States. The 1983 intervention saved not only the students and faculty at St. George's University, but restored order and democracy in a country on the brink of chaos. For that reason, many Grenadians hold the U.S. dear in their hearts.

Compared to the other islands in the region, the U.S. spends an inordinate amount of money in Grenada. There was an American Charge, and four local employees. The U.S. maintained a consular office and a residence for the Charge. Since 9/11, visa issuance had to take place in Barbados, so the work had nearly disappeared. During the budget process, when I suggested it would be much more cost efficient to staff Grenada in the same way we do our other small islands, I was told in no uncertain terms to forget it. Some members of the Congress would not hear of making such a change. *This sentiment costs around $1 million each year.*

Our credential presentation coincided with Grenada National Days. This celebration goes on for several days and is also their Independence Day. Many non-resident members of the diplomatic corps also attended the ceremonies so it was a great opportunity to get acquainted. As part of the government hospitality, we were all loaded on a non air conditioned bus to tour the island, stopping at various facilities the government guide felt were significant. Our first stop was a national forest—a wondrous sight far up in the hills with a lake that had formed inside a long dormant volcano. Local vendors were selling spice leis—fresh nutmeg, ginger, cinnamon, and cocoa beans and they perfumed the air. It was here we encountered our first green monkey. These creatures run wild in most all of the islands. Imported from Africa as pets decades ago, they have multiplied until they are now considered pests. There were a couple of kids in a van eating bananas when the monkeys came out of the trees, jumped into the van, grabbed the bananas, and took off running, leaving the kids screaming in fear. Several of the little creatures sat on the fence, appearing to be posing for pictures.

After the national forest, the roads were all single lane, that lane not really wide enough for a bus. Since there was no air conditioning, the windows on the bus were open, allowing branches of roadside greenery to come through the windows to brush us in the face. We surely hoped we would not meet another vehicle. After a stop at an organic banana production location, where there were no people or bananas to be seen, we were flagged down by several local people, shouting and waving the driver to stop. Some members on the bus muttered "Hijacking," but word was there was a bridge washout ahead. We could not go forward, and there had been no place to turn around, so the driver backed the bus for miles, over very steep hills and hairpin curves with no guard rails. Kay and I whispered to each other "We may have a very short career in the Caribbean!" While backing up, the driver provided a running commentary of points of interest, including a very small chattel type house with no windows and a thatched roof. "That's my pappy's house," he said. Then he stuck his head out the window, waving and yelling "HI PAPPY!" as we backed by. We never saw Pappy. Chattel houses are a Caribbean mobile home, created in times of slavery and indentured servitude. When slaves were sold, or servitude changed, they could take their house apart and take it with them.

Lunch was scheduled for 2 p.m. At 4:30 p.m., still moving in reverse, we finally arrived at the restaurant. The owner and her staff had prepared a wonderful lunch. Everyone enjoyed the multi-course luncheon starting at about 4:30. The iced rum punches were very welcome after that bus ride. After lunch, there was no option but to get back on that bus to return to the hotel. At least we were moving forward this time.

The governor general's reception at the Spice Island Hotel that evening was to be formal. Formal and HOT? The venue was another beautiful hotel, where the crowded ballroom had high ceilings and was located right on the beach, but it was all open to the air, meaning no air conditioning. Thank goodness the governor general departed early. That meant we could too. Back at our hotel there was a lovely breeze off the sea, a local family playing the steel pan drums on the lawn and rum punches available. Life was good!

Next morning our hosts arrived at 7 a.m., to deliver us to our first National Day Celebration. The ceremony was held at the Cricket oval. Cricket is the favorite sport throughout the Caribbean. We were seated in the grandstand under a roof. This became very important, as it poured rain at least three times during the ceremony. In between the showers, the sun came out and the temperature and the humidity both climbed to the 90s. The uniformed participants stood in military order on the field; everyone from the police, firefighters and the military, to the Red Cross, the church youth groups and the Boy Scouts and Girl Guides. These people stood on the field for the entire ceremony, almost three hours. They simply ignored the rain. "Showers of blessing," our hosts told us. However, when the sun came out, it was so hot; people began fainting, just falling down, right and left. Emergency workers were kept very busy.

The governor general reviewed the troops while the police band played. The Venezuelans sent their parachute jumpers to add to the festivities. However, when the practice for the jump took place the previous day, many Grenadians thought they were under attack and bombarded the police stations with calls. Six jumpers were to perform the demonstration jump, but only two actually landed in the stadium. The other four had to be picked up by the police and delivered to the stadium. When they arrived at the stadium, they received a polite round of applause.

At the end of the celebration, the PM made his "state of the country" a speech, largely covering what a great job he and his government were doing. He is a very smart politician. Those who stayed to hear the speech were treated to free box lunches. We declined the box lunch and headed back to the airport for our return to Barbados.

Credential presentation in Dominica provided another great adventure. The final approach to the airport runway in Dominica is through a narrow valley whose steep hillsides are covered with banana trees. I swear if we could have opened the window of the airplane we could have picked bananas on our way down. Then, we learned to pray the brakes were good or we might find ourselves in the Atlantic Ocean, located at the other end of a *very* short runway. The terminal looked like a very small house, but there was a VIP lounge. The lounge was painted bright yellow, with a wall mural depicting an early battle between the Caribs and the Arawaks (early settlers). It had three chairs, a love seat and a three cushion sofa all upholstered in a bright yellow, blue and green fabric. Most important, there was a restroom. This airport was not equipped with lights, so when a flight was delayed and take off could not occur before 6 p.m.; passengers spent the night in Dominica—at the airport. After that first trip, I always announced to the folks who were traveling with me "dibs on the sofa." Fortunately we were never forced to endure an overnight stay at the airport.

The trip from the airport to Roseau, the nation's capital, was about a two hour drive, not many miles, just constant turns and switchbacks through the rain forest. The government always provided a car with a uniformed officer and a security person to meet us at the airport. The driver knew the road well, and when he came to blind curves, he just leaned on the horn until we were around it. We had been warned that if we were susceptible to motion sickness we should load up on medication before leaving the airport. Many first time travelers did not make the trip without nasty car sickness. Fortunately, neither one of us is given to motion sickness, but we held hands and kept our eyes closed most of the way. The road was supposedly two lanes, but it was clear the space available for the road was limited by the jungle greenery. Obviously their asphalt spreader was a one lane machine. So, it was a one lane road through mountainous rain forest, with no guard rails anywhere. WOW. We were very glad to see the lights of Roseau, the capital city, and to arrive at the Ft. Young Hotel. The Ft. Young was actually built inside the old fort, with cannons still in place. The cannons pointed both toward sea and toward the land, apparently to be prepared for attack from any direction.

Our security officer was a somewhat forbidding, large, and mostly silent gentleman. He was greeted in some way by nearly everyone we met. Trying to make conversation, I said, "Everyone seems to know you." He replied "Yes they do.

That's why you are very safe with me. No one takes me on." *OK, perfectly clear.* When we reached our hotel suite, he conducted a complete inspection while we waited in the hallway. He checked the closets, the drawers, under the bed, on the balconies, even in the bathrooms. Even though we did not feel threatened at any time, we felt *absolutely* safe after he nodded, gave an informal salute, and left us alone. It was a beautiful old structure, with huge hanging ferns, blooming succulent plants growing out of the walls of the old fort and springs trickling down to ponds filled with water lilies. Our suite had balconies looking out over the rocky shore. No beaches at this spot, just very large black rocks. That evening we had dinner on the verandah of the hotel with the Roman Catholic bishop of Dominica, one of the youngest bishops in the world. Dominica is predominantly Catholic. He was extremely articulate and well informed on the issues impacting his country and his people. We listened and learned as he shared history, culture, legend and current conditions in a beautifully modulated voice with a delightful British accent. At his urging, we tried several local delicacies, among them callaloo soup. It was a deep grass green, very thick and *really awful*. Otherwise an interesting and delicious meal.

Next morning we presented credentials. Dominica has a president, not a prime minister. His office in his home up in the hills; a lovely setting but a very modest residence. The residence was similar to ones that could be found in any small town or farmstead in Iowa. With scarcely enough space in the room for Kay and me and President Liverpool, the rest of the entourage waited outside. A stark contrast to the huge old government houses on the other islands. President Liverpool shared his concerns for his people. His primary interest was agriculture, and his home was located in the middle of his "farm." Kay and I both enjoyed the visit. It was similar to visiting with my Uncle Clyde or Kay's Uncle Frank. He knew something about Iowa being an agricultural state, and after expressing his concerns about the banana farmers, it became clear he expected me to do something about it. This conversation provided the "other side" of the globalization of the banana business. The banana industry in these small islands consisted mostly of small farmers who harvested and delivered their bananas to the port weekly, where they were paid in cash. This allowed them to pay their bills and their employees, who were mostly family members. This issue affected many of our islands, and will be covered in a later chapter.

Later that morning, we met with the new Prime Minister of Dominica, Roosevelt Skerritt. A handsome and articulate young man, he is a real rock star in his country, and he was extremely unhappy with the U.S. government. He felt he had been promised assistance, which never arrived. After listening to him, I began to understand his position. A group within the State Department, working with Congress, was insisting countries sign an Article 98 agreement with the U.S. I will speak to this issue in a later chapter.

After listening to his concerns, I had to be honest and say I did not know of specific programs or funds we might be able to share. But I gave him my word I would investigate and get back to him within three days. I assured him he had my personal attention. This seemed to be satisfactory. He then shared with me how grateful he was for the fine education he had received in the U.S. as a Fulbright scholar. He had graduated from the University of Mississippi. At the end of our discussion he stood, walked over to where I was standing, gave me a hug and said "God Bless America!" Everyone in the room was shocked. Actually, some of the embassy staff with me thought he was attacking me. Even the more experienced officers present had never seen anything like that. I was touched and heartened by his gesture. That day I gained a new appreciation of just how fragile these small countries can be. Dominica has fewer than 60,000 people, and the main export, bananas, faced a very uncertain future. I also gained a new appreciation of how valuable educating young leaders in America can be.

Later we visited the Coal Pot Soap Factory, a small business producing soap in a small building located in a remote village. A Peace Corps volunteer helped five young women to start this business using all natural ingredients, available to them in their immediate surroundings. This entrepreneurial adventure had so much potential, we'll learn more about it later.

St. Vincent and the Grenadines was next on the credentials list and Peter arrived at 5 a.m. to take us to the airport for our trip. LIAT, the "Leave Island at Any Time" airline, gave us a sample of why the nickname is so apropos. Our flight would be several hours late. Since we were scheduled to leave so early, the VIP lounge was not staffed, Peter did not feel it was appropriate for us to wait in the public departure lounge, so we were headed back to the car. However, the staff at British West Indies Airline (BWIA, "bee-wee") invited us all into their "executive lounge" to wait for our flight, a lovely gesture of hospitality on their part. The governor general was also waiting there, so the problem became an opportunity to have some discussion and continue making friends. Lesson learned: We were never off-duty.

Our hotel in St. Vincent was small, with many steps, no elevator, and a show stopping view of the sea. For breakfast in the morning with our toast we were served warm guava jelly. We ordered more toast so we could eat the whole dish of the stuff. Absolutely addictive.

The credentialing process in St. Vincent was very informal. It took place at the governor general's residence; a beautiful old plantation house set high on a hill to catch the breeze, with a breathtaking view of the sea. We were invited to wait in a colorful room decorated with historic artifacts and with several huge, gorgeous floral arrangements featuring native blooms. When the governor general arrived, we visited for a few minute, then simply exchanged envelopes. There were no speeches; we just visited about a variety of things of mutual interest. He was very generous with time, very hospitable. We learned to choose water when beverages were offered. Much more appealing than the room temperature juice or tea. We still really noticed the heat. Everyone told us we'd become acclimated and we continued to hope it would happen sooner rather than later!

Since Prime Minister Gonsolves was still in New York meeting with Donald Trump, we met with the acting prime minister. He appeared neither interested in nor prepared for our visit, so we didn't stay long.

The Tourism Minister, young, energetic and eager to make friends in the U.S., was assigned to take us to lunch at the Cobblestone Inn. The Inn was on Front Street, one of three named streets in the capital. The other two are Middle Street and Back Street. The Inn was a very old hotel with a rooftop restaurant. There was an awning to protect from the noontime sun, but no fans, so still HOT. As we were being seated, we noticed a table of Americans having lunch. One of them came over and asked, "Aren't you Mary Kramer?" They were from Waterloo, Iowa, neighbors of my Iowa Senate colleague Don Redfern, and they recognized me. The coincidental meeting of fellow Iowans in a small restaurant on St. Vincent created quite a scene. They had spent winters at their property on the Grenadine island of Becquia for over thirty years. Our host Minister was incredibly impressed that we were recognized by Americans in the restaurant in St. Vincent. By the time our lunch arrived we had been introduced to everyone in the restaurant and invited to visit Becquia any time we could come.

The welcome gathering this time was held on Young Island, about a ten-minute boat ride from the main island, in a very small boat that shuttles back and forth. Three young women joined us in the boat, obviously Americans. While visiting with them, I learned they were Peace Corps Volunteers on the island and they were thrilled to be invited to this reception. Even more thrilled when they discovered who I was. They had spent several hours on public transportation to get there and weren't sure how they would get back, but they were so determined to be there they were willing to walk back if they had to. These young volunteers were so enthusiastic, we agreed to visit some of their projects the next day.

The hotel on Young Island consisted of individual cottages set up in the hills. The only common space for the hotel, or on the island itself for that matter, was the restaurant area surrounding the pool. The guests all arrived by boat. Everyone was extremely hospitable and there was lovely food and drink, but it was so crowded one could hardly move. Did I mention it was hot? Many Americans winter on the various Grenadine islands, and they were all very pleased to be included. Clearly it had been years since they met a U.S. ambassador.

The Foreign Minister was in a much better humor and introduced us in a very long, flowery, effusive speech with many compliments, interrupted often by applause. With so much rum punch available and so many people poolside on an uneven flagstone pool deck in so little space, Kay and I were betting that someone would fall into the pool. Thankfully no one did. At the end of the evening, one of the American guests offered to deliver the Peace Corps group back to their homes.

The next day we had lots of appointments. One was with the Catholic bishop who lived in a magnificent residence, high above the sea. The view was breathtaking. He insisted we stay for "tea" and served *very* strong tea and a *very* sweet white cake with lots of sticky pink frosting. During our visit, we could hear the continual crowing of a rooster. With a twinkle in his eye, the bishop told us not to worry about a betrayal if the cock crowed three times. In fact, he told us, "That rooster crows all day and most of the night. It is a confused and annoying bird. Perhaps I will have it for Sunday dinner one day."

We then moved on to "Mesopotamia," a remarkably fertile valley high up in the hills. The numbers of small fields of row crops was amazing. Lots of pumpkins, squash and sweet potatoes. The plowed rows went up and down the steep hillsides instead of in rows of terraces around the hillside. My soil conservationist dad would have been appalled because this method of planting allowed the frequent heavy rains to wash the valuable top soil down to the valleys below. We learned that since the market for bananas had virtually disappeared, many farmers had turned to marijuana as their cash crop, but not where it could be seen from the road.

On to visit the Peace Corps projects. One volunteer, Megan, was locally known as "the tall white girl in the blue shorts." For her project she had taken over an abandoned concrete-block building and converted it to a library and neighborhood center. The governor general donated some comfortable furniture, the neighbors built bookshelves, and a local businessman donated windows. Megan had gathered books and material on a variety of topics including HIV/AIDS from various U.S. sources, so there was lots of reading material available. Paint had also been donated. Since the project was not quite ready for paint, she had stored gallons of it under her bed. We had to visit before five in the evening because there is no electricity in the area and it would be too dark to see. When we arrived many of the neighbors came to greet us. Their pride in their accomplishment was almost unbelievable. Even in its incomplete state, the Center was already being used. We flew back to Barbados that evening with a new appreciation of the value of our young Peace Corps Volunteers. That appreciation has stayed with us to this day.

Next we were off to St. Lucia to present credentials and celebrate National Days. Kay would take a later flight to join me. When I arrived at the hotel, The Royal St. Lucian, I was met by the general manager, who personally escorted me to the Presidential Suite, where champagne and chilled fresh fruit were waiting. He pointed out the Royal Suite, one floor above the Presidential Suite, where the Prince would be in residence for the next several days. He was coming to St. Lucia for National Days. The suite was huge, including a living room, dining area, huge bedroom and bath, plus a deck with potted palms and banana trees that had eight lounge chairs facing the sea, a dining area with a fringed pink and white striped tent capable of seating twelve people for dinner, complete with a crystal chandelier. There was also a hot tub surrounded by potted palm trees! It looked down over the resort beach where there were large round structures with thatched roofs that served as beach umbrellas. The view included the seagoing entrance to Rodney Bay and the yacht harbor which was just past the hotel, so it was wonderful entertainment to watch the coming and going of many huge private vessels. These were very classy accommodations for the "government" rate.

We were scheduled to meet Peace Corps Director Earl Phillips across the street from the hotel at the "Memories of Hong Kong" restaurant for dinner. Earl was a resident of St. Lucia, and served as the Regional Peace Corps Director for six of my islands and was well known on the islands. Barbados had "graduated" economically and was too prosperous to be eligible for Peace Corps Volunteers. Earl became a trusted friend and a valued resource.

The thought occurred to me it was really a shame I couldn't just hang out and enjoy these fabulous accommodations. But the St. Lucian escorts arrived early the next morning to drive me to our meeting with the governor general, Dame Pearlette Louisy. Dame Louisy was a very wise, down-to-earth woman. Since both of us were former educators, we found we had much in common. She was straightforward and knowledgeable about conditions in her country, and openly shared her view of relations with the U.S. She personally admired the U.S. and hoped I could build a more positive relationship with the government. She believed a friendly rapport was not in place at the moment and was sorely needed. She clearly expected to discuss substantive matters and I found our visit together enlightening. I learned much from our visit and looked forward to visiting with her on ensuing visits.

As on the other islands, credential presentations involved lots of protocol and much media coverage. Who knew how many people considered themselves media on these small islands? No matter the numbers; they were very polite and considerate. Quite unlike most of the media I have been used to working with in the U.S. No rude questions! Maybe it was just my honeymoon period.

Since it seemed nearly every government minister in St. Lucia wanted to meet and greet, we had a full day of meetings ahead. At noon, the Venezuelan ambassador, who was the Dean of the St. Lucia diplomatic corps, hosted us for luncheon at her residence. Venezuela, with a long coastline fronting the Caribbean, had resident diplomatic missions in each of these small islands, and they offered free Spanish classes to the island children. Apparently, Hugo Chavez had not found time to move his ambassadors very often because nearly all of them in the Caribbean were women and were "deans" of the local diplomatic corps, meaning they have the longest service of any diplomat in the country. They were all appointed before he came to power. The guest list included my "entourage" and the diplomatic corps resident in St. Lucia, which included the British, the French, the Chinese, and the Cuban. I remembered the protocol; be gracious to the Cuban, but no photos. This Cuban was not particularly nice to me; he just nodded and did not speak, so it was no problem keeping my distance.

After lunch, we left to attend the graduation ceremony for the new class of Peace Corps Volunteers. This was to take place in Soufriere, near the southern tip of the island, at the foot of the magnificent Pitons, the famous twin sugarloaf mountains which were labeled as a world heritage site. The actual distance to Soufriere is only a few actual miles, but with the ups and downs, switchbacks, curves and hills, the trip took almost two hours. The police officer assigned to be our driver/bodyguard knew where he was going and drove, shall we say, aggressively. All the time I was holding on to the armrest remembering I had to come back this way!

It was worth the trip. Peace Corps Volunteers are wonderful people with hearts to serve. I made a few remarks, mostly thanking them for their willingness to serve and then spent about an hour answering questions and getting acquainted with them, all ages, many levels of experience, and several husband/wife teams who were serving their country as part of their retirement. I am once again reminded our country is blessed with wonderful citizens who want to help. I presided over their graduation ceremony. Did I mention it was HOT? The classroom facility was primitive; a cement floor, cement block walls, and a corrugated metal roof. The windows were just openings in the walls, and there was no indoor plumbing.

A group of Roman Catholic nuns provided this facility for Peace Corps training. For the graduation reception, the sisters baked cakes and decorated them with the flags of each of the Caribbean countries where the volunteers would be assigned. The cakes were beautiful, served with warm, red, sweet fruit punch. *Thankfully, it was wet.*

Back over the twisting virtual road to the capital for the evening reception hosted by Earl Phillips at his residence. I met so many people and the house was so crowded, the hospitality was warm in every sense of the word. It was distracting to be continually conscious of the temperature. I hope to acclimate in a hurry.

I was one of very few gray haired white women on these islands and it seemed everyone recognized me and remembered my name. I have now made probably 200 new friends on St. Lucia. Remembering people by name used to be one of my best skills, but when every single person is new, remembering names is tough. None of my memory tricks seemed to work consistently.

It was very late when we arrived back at the hotel, still very hot. So I ordered "gallons" of water and chocolate chip cookies and ice cream from room service and enjoyed the deck and view. I fell asleep on the chaise under the stars, woke up around 3 a.m., and went to bed.

Up early again, this time for breakfast with a Chamber of Commerce type group. They wanted to fill me in on all the things the U.S. had not done for them over the past years, including some bird project that failed more than ten years previous. I put on my endlessly pleasant face and asked what their goals and plans were so we could review them and work together to find support for them. Not surprising, they had no goals and plans. I suggested that when they completed their plans, they could contact the Foreign Service officer who was assigned to St. Lucia, and we would schedule another meeting. We parted great friends. Fortunately that endlessly pleasant thing was working, so I did not say what I was thinking. "Stop whining!" By the way, that next meeting never occurred. The young political officers with me thought I was a genius. They would surely borrow that strategy!

Now I was ready for a fun opportunity. I was scheduled to turn over a Rigid Hull Inflatable Boat (RHIB) to the St. Lucia Marines. Law enforcement in the region really needed the kind of "go fast" power this boat can provide, since all the "bad guys," i.e., drug runners, had them. As always, the media troupe was present. The St. Lucia Marines and the police had collaborated to create quite an event. There was a tent on the pier with a podium and a microphone and rows of folding chairs, filled with lots of government officials. Like politicians everywhere, they don't want to miss a photo opportunity or the chance to speak publicly and get quoted. When it was my turn, I made brief remarks and handed over the keys. The young Marine captain was clearly at a loss for words. Public speaking was obviously not in his skill set. So to relieve his discomfort I said to him, "Don't I get a ride?" His face lit up, and next thing I knew I was bundled into an over-sized orange life jacket. Quickly I was buckled into the "navigator" seat. The seat had a familiar look and feel. It was really a big old fashioned tractor seat mounted on a pole with a spring so it moved with the water and the movement of the boat. We cruised sedately out of the harbor, waving to the spectators as we went by. I knew the boat had a speed capacity of over forty knots. So I asked, "Captain, just how fast is 40 knots?" He grinned and showed me! *Forty knots means flying.* I'm not sure we were even touching the water. This was great!

We arrived safely back at the dock, to the obvious relief of the security officers assigned to me. It was time to return to the hotel and meet Kay. We were due to attend the reception with the prince, on the Royal Navy ship the "HMS Monmouth." Kay was not there. It got later and later and I had no com-munication from anywhere regarding why he was so late or when he might arrive. The phone in my suite didn't work, my cell phone was unable to locate a network, and I was worried. The rest of my group had already left, and the starting time for the reception had long passed. I should have known it would be the vagaries of LIAT (Leave Island At any Time). They had changed the schedule without notice. "No worries," and no communication, either. As it turned out, the prince was delayed too, much to the chagrin of the British commissioner on St. Lucia; he missed the reception in his honor. My team members represented the U.S. without Kay and me.

When Kay finally arrived, it was long past dinnertime, but we were both hungry, so we walked across the street to a restaurant called the BUZZ. It had been highly recommended and correctly so. We had a delicious dinner of fresh pecan-crusted red snapper, so the evening ended well.

Next morning, we toured a development at the north point of the island near the St. Lucia Golf and Country Club. We had learned there was a Rotary charity golf event going on so we stopped by, caused quite a stir and met some lovely local Rotarians. In the development, there were no roads, not even the virtual ones we previously experienced. We toured two beautifully furnished model homes with fabulous views of the sea, but it was fortunate we were being driven in a large four-wheel vehicle. We might not have made it back in a car. Still, after overlooking the site of the proposed new golf course, we had to agree with our guide. When Jack Nicklaus completes the design and the course is completed, it will be even more beautiful than Pebble Beach in California. And with much better weather.

We returned to the hotel in the early afternoon just in time to dress up again and be escorted to the gala evening celebrating National Days. We were driven to the cricket oval and shown to our seats with the rest of the diplomatic corps. We were in the second row, behind the prime minister and his wife, the governor general, and the prince. The invitation said "Formal, Black Tie." So Kay, being fully prepared, wore his white dinner jacket and black bow tie.

Did I mention it was really HOT? Anyway, every other man there was either in full military uniform, or in dark business suit and tie. Kay said, "I felt like the Pillsbury Doughboy on parade!"

First order of business for the evening, the governor general and His Royal Highness, Duke of York reviewed the troops. Once again, every group on the island that had uniforms formed up for the review. The governor general was resplendent in her white suit and a really smashing white hat. The prince was in his full-dress white uniform, complete with gold shoulder epaulets and a handsome saber. The St. Lucia Police Band played the ever-popular "Yellow Bird" while everyone marched by the reviewing stand, slow march and then quick time. Then they lined up on the cricket oval and the governor general and the Prince walked among them. All this required many repetitions of "Yellow Bird."

After the troop review, we were treated to a Las Vegas-type show. Gorgeous and extravagant costumes, dancing, loud music and many acts, each depicting the long and glorious history of St Lucia. It was a great show. Just too much of it. Way too much. In fact, as the evening wore on, people around us began falling asleep. The French ambassador usually wore two pairs of glasses when he was reading, and was very fond of his cell phone and his Blackberry. When he dozed off, both pairs of glasses, his cell phone and his Blackberry all crashed loudly to the floor. Shortly after, Prince Andrew must have dozed off as well because his sword clattered to the floor, bringing the security officers to full attention. Being newbies, we stayed till the evening ended, nearly 1:30 a.m. After all, protocol dictates we should not leave before the governor general. When we stood to go and turned around there were only empty seats behind us. Apparently, only members of the diplomatic corps were bound by protocol. Staff members and local citizens had long since deserted the field.

The next morning, the National Day celebration was scheduled to continue at 7 a.m., and our invitation noted that we were to be seated by 6:45 a.m. Supposedly this was so the ceremony would be finished before the day got too warm. As we expected, the festivities were on Caribbean time. They got underway about an hour late, and went on for at least 90 minutes. Speeches, parade review, etc. As in Grenada, there were many opportunities for the local Emergency Responders group to demonstrate their readiness and enthusiasm for rescue, because people on the field kept collapsing from the heat. There was a very nice continental breakfast served in a tent adjoining the field after the ceremony. Did I mention it was HOT? Then off to the airport. Our plane was three hours late, but thankfully the VIP lounge at the airport was air-conditioned. It provided a nice opportunity to visit with other diplomats who had attended the ceremonies.

Our dear friends from Iowa, the Rosonkes, arrived for their first visit about the time Kay was ready to escape back to the States. He needed some familiar faces for company. I was scheduled to present credentials in St. Kitts, so Kay stayed behind to meet the Rosonkes. They planned to fly to St. Kitts to join me the next day. When I arrived in St. Kitts, I was met at the airport by an attractive young woman protocol officer and the uniformed policeman who was the driver. It was pouring rain, with the temperature well over 90 degrees, surely 90 percent humidity as well. Although the vehicle was not air conditioned, the car windows remained closed to avoid drenching the passengers. That car was my first experience in a moving sauna.

I was driven to the magnificent new St. Kitts Marriott Resort and Casino. I was greeted at the front entrance by the general manager, who escorted me to Suite 500, the Presidential Suite. I was the very first occupant. It had a large living room and a dining room with capacity to seat 16 people. There was a long marble buffet counter laden with platters of fruit, cheese and crackers, with both red and white wines chilling. The suite had two bedrooms, each with lavish bath. Every room had sliding glass doors that opened onto a balcony, each with an ocean view. The island of Nevis was visible in the distance. Since I was alone with all this grandeur and there were bountiful food and drink, I called the staff who accompanied me and said "Come on up, let's have a party." Of course they were delighted to do so. I couldn't wait for Kay and the Rosonkes to arrive to share this fabulous accommodation.

Next morning, my first appointment was with Governor General Cuthbert to present my credentials. His residence is another beautiful old plantation style house with the now familiar larger than life oil painting of Queen Elizabeth II in her younger days. Governor General Cuthbert was such a substantial man he couldn't fit into a standard-sized chair, so he had a large throne-like chair in his formal living room. I noticed later that wherever he went, his entourage carried a large chair for him. He was charming and had a great sense of humor. Our conversation consisted mainly of his detailed description of his knighthood ceremony at Buckingham Palace, clearly the highlight of his life. In his younger days he practiced medicine on St. Kitts and Nevis and had delivered most of the babies born on St. Kitts and Nevis for many years. A beloved figure.

At our next appointment, I could not help but notice the contrast. Prime Minister Denzil Douglas was a small, fit man who was a track champion while attending college in the U.S., and had represented St. Kitts in the Olympics. He too was a medical doctor. He was passionate about his country's needs and very unhappy with the U.S. government. The attorney general was with him in the meeting, having been forewarned that I wanted to discuss the potential extradition of two American drug kingpins living on the island. Both the prime minister and the attorney general insisted that the men were still free because they hadn't exhausted their legal remedies. Their government could not extradite them until all legal options were completed. I asked, "How long has this legal battle been going on?" "Ten years," was the response. "And how many more appeals are available to them?" I asked. "Just one," was the response. "And since it is the third time the Privy Council has heard their case, are they likely to win this time?" The answer. "Not a chance." "So, can we expect your government to act expeditiously when the Privy Council decision is announced?" Both men shook their heads doubtfully, looked down, and said they would have to get back to me on that. I explained that it would be difficult for me to do business with a government that continues to harbor known criminals. I told them my expectations were that the two would be dealt with properly as soon as the final court decision was known. We enjoyed some pleasant small talk after that, with friendly handshakes on parting.

Back at the hotel, I learned that Kay and the Rosonkes were stranded in the Antigua airport. LIAT struck once again. The Antigua airport would never be known as a comfortable place to wait, but they had discovered an air conditioned restaurant on the second level called the Big Banana, so all was well. I was disappointed they would not arrive in time for the evening reception.

The welcome reception on St. Kitts took place in another beautiful setting, a hotel deck high above the beach, with cool breezes and not a cloud in the sky. A beautiful evening, nice steel pan music, and a big crowd. The Dean of Ross University, an American Veterinary College on St. Kitts, graciously hosted the event. I met many Americans who taught at the university, local business owners and property owners, and a variety of people who just enjoy the Caribbean and spend time on St. Kitts. Many varied ideas and opinions were shared, and I listened and learned.

By the time I returned to the hotel, Kay and the Rosonkes had finally arrived. Everyone was suitably impressed with the suite. It was still early in the evening, so we decided to explore the hotel and ended up in the lobby bar where there was an excellent musical group performing. The bar menu listed four pages of exotic drinks. That was the first and only time in my years at Post that I had a drink with a little umbrella in it.

Next morning, I met the St. Kitts Ambassador to the U.S. for breakfast at the hotel. A Canadian-educated psychiatrist, he had been kind enough to attend my swearing-in ceremony in Washington. He ordered something called ackee for breakfast. Fortunately I was not very hungry because it looked and smelled awful, resembling the Caribbean version of Norwegian lutefisk. He relished every bite. I had toast. He was a great admirer of Iowa Senator Charles Grassley, of University Extension Services, and of the 4-H. He believed the introduction of 4-H clubs and extension services, along with reactivating the

Peace Corps on St. Kitts, would be most valuable for his country. Since I am from Iowa where both 4-H and University Extension Services are highly successful, he was supremely confident I would be able to get all that done during my term of service. I thanked him for his confidence in me.

Several years earlier, St. Kitts' law enforcement efforts had become so problematic for Americans the Peace Corps had withdrawn all their volunteers and closed the office on St. Kitts. Prior to my arrival, an American student at Ross University had been murdered, and law enforcement experts at the Embassy told me the investigation was so badly bungled that it was highly unlikely the murderer would ever be caught. Skills and training were lacking among members of law enforcement, and even more distressing, there seemed to be little interest in learning. Apparently the withdrawal of the Peace Corps Volunteers had sent a serious message, and St. Kitts' government had become concerned enough that the leaders of local law enforcement requested training classes and materials from U.S. military and Narcotics Affairs personnel. As a result, the skill level and the motivation to respond had definitely improved. The Dean of the Veterinary School told me he had seen marked improvement of response by police to calls from his students and staff. The new Marriott resort was designed to attract large numbers of American and Canadian tourists, so the government understood that competent and responsive law enforcement was critical to encouraging tourism.

The change in attitudes and the results gained through the training experiences caused the Peace Corps officials to agree to reopen an office on a trial basis. Much to the delight of everyone, a new group of Peace Corps Volunteers had arrived and was ready to begin work. Everyone was on notice to give personal attention to the security and safety of these volunteers. So, later that day, Earl Phillips, the regional director of the Peace Corps in the Caribbean, the governor general (with his own chair), the prime minister, a Peace Corps representative from Washington, and I presided over a large and formal ceremony that included numerous speeches about the importance of the Peace Corps and a ribbon-cutting for the reopening of the office. It was a very big tent. The new class of Peace Corps Volunteers presented a clever skit with music and percussion. Did I mention there were many lengthy speeches and it was really hot? Still, it was a very festive occasion. Kay and the Rosonkes were suitably impressed. Following the ceremonies, everyone went upstairs to the new office for fruit punch, chicken wings, stuffed eggs, and perfectly trimmed triangular sandwiches with mysterious fillings.

Before leaving Washington I learned that the Premiere of Nevis was leading an attempt to secede from that island's federation with St. Kitts. The U.S. government was opposed to this move since the total population of

Nevis numbered around 9,000, including winter residents. He seemed immune to communication about the folly of this idea. *Perhaps a man who would be king?*

The business community of St. Kitts and Nevis was a united group, leading some very effective economic development work. During my meeting with the business leaders of both islands, I learned the entire business community was also opposed to this separation. My sense of humor got the better of me and during the discussion I said, "It appears to me that this is a solution looking for a problem." They all applauded. Oops! Be careful with that spontaneous sense of humor. Fortunately no media were present.

Later that evening I met with the leader of the opposition party. He was a fiery, passionate, and articulate young man. His critique of the present government, and his plans for winning future elections, reminded me that partisanship is pretty much the same everywhere. After the business of the day concluded, around 9 p.m., I enjoyed a quiet dinner with Kay and the Rosonkes. Kay and I enjoyed a real American steak, our first since leaving Iowa. During dinner, an excellent local musician played the saxophone near our table. During a conversation with him, we learned he lived in Nevis and grew the organic lettuce that supplied the hotel restaurants. For fun, he performed in the steakhouse. In the small world department, it turned out he was the cousin of the opposition party leader I had just met and he had already heard about the meeting. Just like Iowa. Better tell the truth because everyone is related to everyone else.

Next morning we were off to Nevis. The general manager of the Four Seasons sent a launch to pick us up. I knew Mary Ann Rosonke sometimes had a bit of a problem with motion sickness, so I had warned her, and she was wearing her motion sickness bands and had her pills in hand. She was fine. The two crew members were real comedians, which kept our minds off a very bouncy ride. However, one of the junior officers in the group spent the entire trip hanging over the side of the boat. He was fine when we docked, but thoroughly embarrassed. No problem, he got some soda and was good to go. We were greeted on the dock and escorted to our room. The hotel lived up to the world class reputation of Four Season Hotels everywhere. A bottle of chilled champagne and a large conch-shaped white china bowl filled with chocolate-dipped strawberries awaited us in our room. The final perfect touch; the bowl was presented on a large plate that was painted in chocolate saying "Welcome to the U.S. Ambassador." Heady stuff!

Kay and the Rosonkes enjoyed the beautiful setting and the beach while I went to present credentials to the Deputy Governor General of Nevis in his old brick home located next to the Alexander Hamilton Museum. Hamilton was born on and spent much of his childhood in Nevis. The museum was in

Hamilton's childhood home, and the Nevis Parliament met upstairs. The deputy governor general was a big fan of Richard Nixon and proceeded to give me his version of U.S. history regarding the Nixon presidency. I was not well versed on that period of our history, but fortunately he did not expect a response. The next meeting was with the premier (not a prime minister) of Nevis and his cabinet. We met in the white clapboard building that housed their government offices. Actually the meeting room itself was smaller than the city council meeting room in Clive. Like many city councils back in the U.S., they were mostly interested in roads, law enforcement and health clinics. Most of the health care facilities and the schools are located on St. Kitts. The Nevisians, of course, would prefer to have their own. The Premier spoke at length of their desire to secede from the federation with St. Kitts. I shared the U.S. government's position with them and made it very clear that the U.S. government had no interest in providing support to Nevis as a separate nation. A difficult message, but I spoke very plainly. I could tell by their body language they didn't believe me. Later we toured the island and visited a small American medical school. A big surprise. Who knew there was one? It was American run, with American faculty and students, and we enjoyed the visit.

The Nevis welcome reception was held at the Botanical Gardens. A truly beautiful setting, and one that was only accessible over a virtual road through a totally uninhabited rain forest. No matter, there was a large attendance, including both the premier and the deputy governor general.

We met many interesting Americans in Nevis. They run hotels, write books, and make jams, jellies, and other craft items to sell in the hotels and at the airport. I met a memorable 104-year-old woman who came to the reception with her daughter. I complimented her on her beauty and she asked me if I knew the secret to beautiful skin. *Apparently not.* Her secret? Never in her life had she taken a bath or washed her face in hot water—not ever. Does foregoing hot water seem a high price for such beauty and longevity. Maybe. But remember, it never gets below 75 degrees on Nevis.

Kay and I spent the night at the Four Seasons. Next morning we had an early breakfast with a group of Americans who form a chapter of Republicans Abroad. Another surprise. Who knew there was such an organization? About 25 people attended, and everyone had a question. Or two. I also met a precocious 11-year-old girl, the daughter of the hostess, who drew me pictures and stayed by my side the entire time. She referred to herself as my mini-republican and presented me with a small clay turtle she had made as a souvenir of my visit. I still have it. Her mother is the warden, a position that is called on to perform American citizen services when they are needed on Nevis. When they learned I was going to be visiting Nevis, they invited me to speak to their group and were willing to schedule their gathering any time I could come. We told them

I was the ambassador for all Americans so my remarks would not be partisan. I would love to have been invited to visit with Democrats abroad as well, but never had the opportunity.

After breakfast there was a radio interview scheduled; turned out to be a call-in show. I again stated clearly that the U.S. government did not favor and would not support a separate state of Nevis. I heard later that after this public announcement, the members of the Nevis government believed me.

On the way back to Barbados, there was another long layover in Antigua. This time, we walked across the gardens adjacent to the airport to a restaurant called the Sticky Wicket. The area surrounding the airport in Antigua was beautiful, with several very large and attractive buildings housing the financial institutions of Allan Stanford, the American millionaire. Mr. Stanford has been in the news more recently for financial problems involving ponzi schemes with those institutions. Our table overlooked a beautiful new cricket oval where a Caribbean version of little league was going on. The field was covered with several hundred boys and girls in colorful t-shirts, being coached on the fundamental skills of cricket.

After arriving back in Barbados, Kay enjoyed exploring Barbados with the Rosonkes while I went to work. Kay had practiced driving on the "wrong" side for a few days and was quite comfortable behind the wheel. He really enjoyed his role as official tour guide. However, they did get lost one afternoon while trying to locate some of the famous "black-belly sheep" we had heard so much about. These animals actually looked like goats. They are easily recognizable because the top of their body is brown and their belly is black. They make delicious lamb chops. After finding their way back toward home, they spied several of these animals tethered in a yard about two blocks from the residence.

We almost missed our six-week presentation goal because elections were being held on Antigua and there were rumors there might be a change of government. It would not have been prudent to present credentials to the current government on the eve of an election. Good thing. After 25 years and several generations of the Byrd family being in power, the Antiguans elected a new government.

We gave the new government a week or so to settle in and then made our final presentation trip. This time we were invited to stay at the American-owned resort, Curtain Bluff. Obviously we had stayed at some of the finest resorts in the Eastern Caribbean, but this one was the epitome of ambiance and service. The American owners not only had a five star resort, they were renowned for caring for their employees. They provided musical instruments and instruction for the children of employees. They provided college scholarships at schools in the U.S. The gentleman who escorted us to our suite had children who graduated from

Iowa Wesleyan College in Mt. Pleasant, Iowa. The gentleman's alma mater! His stories describing his first visit to Iowa to see his children were hilarious. It was winter and no one had prepared him for the cold. He was convinced his children would be "crying to come home." They weren't, but he was!

Curtain Bluff was truly one big happy family and a model of positive investment in a small country. The owners' close ties to their employees, the educational scholarships, provision of music lessons, etc., led to a high esprit de corps among the staff, and in the surrounding neighborhoods as well. The hotel community was in a rather remote location on Antigua, but it was noticeably more prosperous than other villages.

Our first evening on Antigua was especially memorable because Juliet and Sven Ryder hosted us for dinner at their home, high above English Bay. Juliet is an American citizen who served as the U.S. consular agent on Antigua. She had provided American citizen services for almost 15 years. She performed a great service to our country. It was her insight and communication that was crucial in identifying the Maryland sniper. He was a person who had spent time on Antigua. That evening, the Ryders sent a hired a van and driver to deliver us from Curtain Bluff to their home. On the map, it seemed a very short distance, but we were told to allow at least an hour for the ride. More virtual roads. No street lamps, only dim lights in a few of the small homes we passed; it became obvious not all of them were equipped with electricity or running water. Kay and I confessed to each other later that night that when the driver turned to go up the final hill leading to the Ryder's residence, we thought we had been hijacked. The old van climbed up over a rutty path through a jungle, cutting through tree limbs that met across the road, trying to avoid huge boulders jutting out of the road surface every few feet. We just kept creeping forward. Then suddenly we were there. The Ryder's beautiful home, pool, and gardens were nestled in the hills high over Nelson's Bay. Sven Ryder was a Norwegian gentleman and a lifelong sailor. His family history and his career were involved with the Norwegian Cruise Lines. As we looked down on English Harbor from the verandah, Sven pointed out many of the yachts anchored in the harbor. Notable among them were vessels belonging to J. Paul Getty and Bill Gates. They were the size of cruise ships, complete with tenders and helipads.

The Ryder's home was decorated with gorgeous collections of antiques collected from their families. The table was set with beautiful linens, china, glassware, and silver, and we were served a fabulous prime rib dinner. Truly a memorable evening.

Next morning we presented credentials to the Antiguan Governor General. This was a formal presentation, followed by a lovely reception.

Sven had invited Kay to join him and his friends at golf, so I asked Juliet to accompany me. The governor general's wife was also in attendance. She had read my biography and knew I had an interest in child care, and she wanted to visit about it. I shared some of the ideas we found useful and she actually implemented some of these ideas and would subsequently call me for advice. A shared interest that served both of us well.

Then, it was off to meet with the new Prime Minister of Antigua, Baldwin Spencer. He was a very large man, as was his predecessor, so everything in this elegant office was large-scale. Huge overstuffed sofas and chairs. A person my size could get lost in them. I sat at the very edge of my chair to avoid slouching or tugging at my skirt, and so my feet would touch the floor. It's difficult to stay focused unless one's feet are on the floor. The PM thanked me profusely for waiting until after election to present my credentials and meet the new government. He confessed that he was fearful that had we come to call on the previous government, it would have appeared the U.S. supported the old government and could have influenced the election. The rest of the day was spent visiting various government officials. One of our stops was the election commission. The group had received very high marks for the way they handled the election and the subsequent change of government. The commission itself was located in a building that had once been an American embassy. We were told it served very well, nothing had been changed, and they were still using furniture that had been left behind at least thirty years before. The Chairman of the commission told me he was sitting at a U.S. ambassador's desk and in a U.S. ambassador's chair. Must have been very high quality stuff; it still looked pretty good.

That evening, the owners of Curtain Bluff hosted the welcome reception for us at their home. Kay and I have had the opportunity to attend many lovely occasions in stunning settings, but this was almost too beautiful to be true. The home sat at the peak of the bluff on a rock formation surrounded on three sides by the sea. Looking into the sunset, one could see the smoke arising in the distance from the live volcano on Montserrat. It was easy to understand why the home had been featured in Architectural Digest. Lavish flower arrangements were beautifully designed with native blooms and greenery. The collection of Caribbean art was gorgeous.

The entire cabinet of the Spencer government attended with spouses and friends. Our hosts and the other Americans present were dumbfounded. This had never happened before. I wondered if the new ambassador or the house was the bigger attraction. Whatever, their presence boded well for our relationship with the new government in the future.

During the reception, we heard a great story about solving problems. The owner of Curtain Bluff had people who painstakingly clean up his beaches several times a day. They are pristine. During one of those cleanups a lot of waste material was found, much of it bearing the logo of a well-known cruise line that made regular stops in Antigua. The cruise business is very important to the country, so he knew he would not receive much assistance from the government in confronting the cruise line. So, he took matters into his own hands. He had his crew put all the garbage bearing the logos in several big garbage bags and tied red bows on them. He then hired the sightseeing helicopter to fly over the departing ship and drop the garbage bags on one of its outdoor decks. He never saw anything from a cruise line on his beach again. *Truth or fiction?* Hard to tell, but either way a great story.

Back in Barbados, it was time to catch our breath and celebrate. After a six-week whirlwind of travel to all seven islands, we had achieved the goal. Credential presentations were complete. First mission accomplished.

I considered the time, money, and energy we spent presenting credentials as an investment, and I was counting on it to deliver huge returns. It absolutely did. The idea of personally visiting each country so promptly after arrival, meeting with people from all walks of life who were surprised and grateful to be acknowledged and listened to, earned me the respect of the people and opened doors that otherwise might have taken half my term to crack.

CHAPTER FIVE

A FLURRY OF FIRSTS AND AN UNWELCOME AHA!

Between credential presentations and early visitors, settling in to our residence had taken a back seat. We had managed to get a car for Kay, but we had no cable television (only the two government stations). We had no way to make international phone calls so we could call home (personal calls were not allowed on the government telephone system), we needed to get connected to the Internet so we could send and receive emails. We had been in country for over six weeks. Kay had a car and it was licensed and insured, but none of the other things had been accomplished. Obviously we needed to apply some pressure and get some help. There seemed to be about a thousand things that had to happen simultaneously.

Thankfully we were already welcoming visitors from home. I was fully engaged in work, so Kay often found himself at the residence with nothing to do. He had been very involved in his consulting practice, served on several boards of directors and had many friends with many planned activities. So with no international phone contacts, no email connections, or cable television (especially the Golf Channel), he was truly bored. We decided to treat ourselves to membership at Sandy Lane Golf Club, so we could play when we were able, but Kay had no ready-made group of friends to call. When he was unhappy and bored, I was unhappy for him. We had been together almost fifty years, and he had cheerfully dropped everything to come along on this great adventure, but we were not used to being bored.

One morning Kay went outside and asked David, our gardener, for tools to wash his car. David looked horrified, and Rita Bowen flew out the back door. "Oh no, Mr. Kramer," Rita said. "We cannot have a dirty car in the ambassador's car park, but this is never for you to do." While Kay was appreciative of the service, he once again wondered what there was for him to do.

Entertaining friends from back home really helped. Throughout our years abroad, Kay was kept busy with visiting friends and family from mid-October through mid-May during our entire stay. Still, it was a much bigger adjustment for him than for me. I had a real job that kept me engaged well over 40 hours per week. Kay did not know anyone and except when he accompanied me, he was not occupied.

We were told it was the expected thing for us to host a welcome reception. Nearly 350 people accepted our invitation for cocktails. The backyard of the CMR was outfitted with huge red and white striped tents. Gorgeous red, white, and blue flower arrangements were delivered, Marines were practicing their flag presentation, the driver crew was figuring out parking logistics, and a band of steel pan players were set to provide just the right amount of sound. Buffet tables were set up all over the grounds with artistic displays of fresh fruits and vegetable trays. During the planning for the party, I learned that certain local specialties, including fish balls, "stuffed" eggs, pumpkin fritters, and fresh shrimp were considered absolutely essential to an appropriately lavish "official" party. Rita Bowen and Kay Hinds, the protocol officer at the embassy, became the arbiters of culturally appropriate "taste" for the Ambassador's Residence, and we were delighted to rely on their judgment. I wanted to entertain graciously, and make sure people felt welcome and enjoyed themselves, but I did not want us to appear to be over the top rich, arrogant Americans.

On the big evening, the weather was perfect, with a full moon over the Caribbean and the temperature hovering about 80 degrees. Kay and I, along with DCM Marcia, Military Liaison Officer and Coast Guard Commander Chris Sinnett, and Pat Shapiro, the USAID Director, made up the receiving line. I was first in line to greet our guests and then introduced them to Kay, who passed them on to Marcia, etc. Kay Hinds stood near me and made brief introductions of many of the guests. We greeted people in a steady stream for over an hour. I disappeared for a minute or so and nearly gave Kay Hinds a heart attack, *but I simply had to change my shoes.* My feet were killing me! Bare feet were certainly not an acceptable option, and there were at least three hours of party to go.

After the flow of arrivals became a trickle, we moved to the backyard for the evening program, which included Kay and I greeting guests with welcoming remarks. A smaller tent, complete with chandelier and a speaker's podium, had been placed on an elevated platform near the backyard pool. The prime minister, the governor general and his wife, Foreign Minister Billie Miller and Attorney General Mia Mottley were all on the platform with Kay and me. The Marines, in full dress blues, presented the flag with precision and respect while the Barbados Police Band played The Star Spangled Banner. Kay and I both were so choked up we had to take a minute to catch our breath before continuing the program. Kay served as master of ceremonies, welcoming people to our home and acknowledging our honored guests. That was a big risk (with his sense of humor, and his lack of "reverence," who knew what he might say). Of course, he was the perfect host. He introduced me and I reiterated how pleased we were to be in Barbados, to have made so many new friends so quickly and how much I looked forward to working together to achieve our mutual goals. Spontaneously, I turned to the prime minister and asked if he would like to address the crowd. I told him "I'm a retired politician; this is really your crowd. It would be a shame to miss an opportunity to say a few words." To say I surprised him would be a massive understatement. I shocked him. Apparently being asked to speak "off the cuff" is not the "done" thing. But he rose to the occasion and clearly enjoyed joking with me and our guests. Whew. What was probably a major protocol error on my part turned out to be a big win. He loved it. Rita told us later we should be so pleased because of the large number of government officials who attended our event. She had been working at the ambassador's residence for many years and had never seen that kind of attendance. We knew we had a very successful launch. Actually, more than 400 of our "new best friends" attended; many more than had officially accepted the invitation. Almost immediately after the speeches, people began to leave so Kay and I were back in the "farewell" line. *Feet still hurting!*

At my first official meeting with Prime Minister Owen Arthur following the welcome reception, he told me how much he enjoyed the party and his chance to speak, and said he would be happy to attend more events at the CME. Good news there. Then he proceeded to counsel me for more than hour on the importance of trade and economic growth to the region. He left no doubt our goals were compatible. He also offered some useful advice:

- Get involved with the entire island community, not just the members of the diplomatic corps or other Americans.

- Trade is of paramount importance. He was trying to unite the English-speaking Caribbean islands into a common market and would appreciate anything we could do to forward that agenda.

- He looked forward to working with a Republican U.S. administration. He told me that many people would doubt both his ability and his desire to work with a Republican president or ambassador, for that matter, because of his strong Labor Party background. He emphatically shared his belief that he and I would get on well together. He knew the U.S./Barbados relationship was not the best, and he would work with me to improve that. Happily, this was becoming a recurring theme from those I met.

This was excellent advice and insight, and provided for a hospitable and sub-stantive first meeting. Clearly his advice and my objectives were aligned nicely.

The prime minister spoke very rapidly and with a heavy Bajan accent. I had to pay close attention to stay with the conversation. Fortunately, my team was with me. Marcia, as well as a trade officer, a military rep, and at least one note-taker from the political office were also present. It made for quite an entourage, but the PM. had an equal number of his folks at the table. He dominated the conversation. He made it very clear that he wanted me to be successful in my new job. At the end of the meeting, the note-taker was exhausted!

During those early days and weeks, it became obvious that my biographi-cal information had been widely reviewed and my years of business experience and my service as an elected official raised expectations that I would be actively involved. Amazing what having been through campaigns and winning elections does for one's credibility with elected officials. The early high energy approach to meeting people and presenting credentials added to that impression. As a result we felt very welcome and ready to do business almost immediately.

Kay and I both wanted to continue our participation in the Rotary Club. Rotary is an international service organization that does good work throughout the world. It was a great way to meet local people, other than government of-ficials, to volunteer and to integrate ourselves into the society. The first time we tried to attend a Rotary meeting even Peter couldn't find the location. They had apparently changed meeting venues for the day. So we went to the clubhouse at Sandy Lane for lunch instead. Sandy Lane was one of the highest ranked resorts in the world. Very expensive and very exclusive; Tiger Woods was married there. But on our first visit, we enjoyed a lovely lunch with a gorgeous view over-looking the Caribbean and the golf course. Being out of doors all the time in this beautiful place was wonderful but came with risks. I leaned back in the elegant upholstered chair, right into fresh bird poop. The poor waitress was appalled and took my jacket away to try to repair the damage. They did a pretty good job of cleaning it, but I was still uncomfortable putting it back on. Yuck!

Our second attempt to attend a Rotary meeting was successful, and we walked in to a regular weekly luncheon. As we arrived and introduced ourselves, it immediately became obvious there were no women members in this club. *Oops.* The club leadership could be seen with their heads together in a private discussion deciding what to do with me. I was not only the U.S. am-bassador; I was a visiting Rotarian as well. They were extremely gracious and hospitable, and invited both of us to sit at the head table. The club president made a lovely introduction and welcomed us. Kay decided he would visit all three of the clubs on the island before deciding where to join, but he settled on the group where we made our first visit. I contemplated pushing the "gender" issue for membership, but as much as I would have enjoyed it, I decided that battle was not one that would be appropriate for the U.S. ambassador to take on. When Kay joined, the group invited me to become an "Honorary Member," so all was well (for me). Still, other women were not invited to participate. However, at the annual meeting of the club in July, the new president initiated the discussion of admitting women members. With some dissension, the group voted to begin accepting women members. By the time we left the islands, there were a number of women members fully participating.

Rotary introduced us to a wonderful circle of friends, opportunities for enjoyable social activities and an easy entry into the society of the islands. We participated in social events and volunteered at various Rotary activities. When we travelled together, Kay visited Rotary Clubs on all of our islands, and as time went on, I was often invited to speak to their meetings. Always a warm welcome and an important audience to hear our message of economic growth and individual liberty.

It was great fun to shock people by showing up as volunteers at Rotary occasions. For example, all the clubs on the island sponsored a large Christmas celebration called Candlelight and Carols. The prime minister generously allowed the event to be held on the grounds of his residence. Kay and I volunteered to sell sandwiches and pour soda. People lined up not only to get their sandwich and soda, but to see the U.S. ambassador acting in this volunteer role. Our security officers were concerned and accompanied us, but it was a really great opportunity for me to model the "friendly" American. Plus, I enjoyed doing it.

The prime minister invited us to attend a cricket match and to sit in his box. British High Commissioner (HC) John White was there as well. HC White was a lifelong student of the game and an excellent tutor. We learned there are one day matches and five day matches. Sometimes in the five day match a single batter might be up to bat for the entire day. And at the end of five days, it is possible for the match to end in a tie. We decided cricket will likely never be an American favorite. Too much spectator patience is required.

We also learned that cricket is indeed a "civilized" sport. The umpires wore button down dress shirts, neckties and straw hats, mostly in white. The matches began about 10 a.m. Peter dropped us off shortly before ten and we enjoyed a continental breakfast with tea and pastries. Then around one o'clock, the teams left the field. During the hour intermission that ensued, we were served lunch. The teams returned to the field around 2 p.m and the match resumed until about 4:30 p.m., when the teams again left the field. During that intermission, we enjoyed high tea, or a rum punch if one preferred. The teams returned to the field and played until dark, around 6 p.m. When the sun goes down, everyone goes home, only to return the next morning to continue the match. A lovely way to spend the day at the Cricket Oval. Even though the sport is civilized, the spectators greatly resemble National Football League fans; passionate for their team. It is a circus atmosphere: vendors, team colors, and paraphernalia, cheers and boos as appropriate.

A USAID sponsored course designed to build trade capacity skills in policy makers and business leaders was about to begin, and I was invited to speak at the opening ceremonies. This was a much anticipated program and was oversubscribed. The auditorium at the University of West Indies (UWI) was packed. The opening ceremonies provided me an informal opportunity to meet Attorney General Mia Mottley, who was also a speaker that day. An imposing woman, always impeccably dressed, she was an outstanding speaker. I was envious of her deep, nearly baritone voice. Like Dame Billie, she was reputed to harbor a very low opinion of the U.S., so I was carefully formal during our brief conversation before the meeting began. However, during her remarks, which followed mine, she made very flattering comments about my background and indicated that she looked forward to working with me. Afterward, I thanked her for her kind remarks and told her I hoped we would become colleagues.

Very special guests were coming to visit, Becky and Charlie Beach. Becky was the assistant who tracked me down at Hilton Head for the all important phone call that began this great adventure, and Charlie and Kay had enjoyed many rounds of golf together.

On a Saturday afternoon during Becky and Charlie's visit, the four of us played golf at Sandy Lane. On the 16th tee, Kay hit a great drive down the fairway, just a little to the right and close to some trees. While we were driving to the ball, a large monkey came out onto the fairway. He picked up Kay's ball, studied it carefully, smelled it, then put it down and leisurely returned to the jungle. We were laughing so hard, we just could not believe what we'd seen. Charlie told Kay "Kramer, if you didn't play with such cheap golf balls, he would have taken it along!" Our second green monkey sighting.

Paul Altman had invited Kay to play in the charity golf tournament at Royal Westmoreland Golf Club to benefit the Duke of Edinburgh Foundation. When Paul learned we had guests from America, he invited them too. So Kay, Charlie, and Becky enjoyed the day of golf, and the dinner that followed at the Club House with Ian Woosnam and Luciano Pavarotti in attendance, was fabulous. Woosnam had a home on the golf course and Pavarotti was a frequent visitor to the island. Everyone that played was presented a really lovely watch. personalized for the occasion. Most important, and *alert the media*, Kay and Charlie won crystal. Four beautiful highball glasses etched with the logo of the tournament.

They reached an agreement; we would display them in the residence until we returned home and then Charlie would take custody. This event was a great opportunity for Kay to meet the island golfing community. Many of the people he met that day later became friends and golfing partners.

In Barbados, there were two daily newspapers, *The Advocate* and *The Nation*. Their readership was extremely high. The government operated two information channels on television, and talk radio was big. I knew this was true because we heard the radio in the residence kitchen almost every day, and from time to time Peter would suggest I listen to the topic of the day while we were driving. I also knew it was true that the embassy had been in the news way too often because of terrible customer service in the consular area. Unfortunately, much of the criticism was well deserved. Fortunately, new Consul General Bob Fretz, had already improved the functioning of the consulate, so there had been relatively little negative media coverage about America since I arrived. Public Diplomacy staff suggested it would be a good idea to entertain members of the media at a get-acquainted lunch at the residence. In the U.S., some media would likely not accept such an invitation, and those that did would be extremely critical. However, I was assured that Barbados media would welcome the opportunity and they did. They were very curious to meet me, and I was eager to share my belief that free and inquiring media is a necessary component of a democratic society. I also wanted to share my feelings about their obligation to be accurate. This occasion provided an opportunity to interview me en masse.

Everyone who was invited came. They arrived at 11:30 a.m. and they all stayed until after 3 p.m. It was a great opportunity for me to informally talk about my charge to maintain stable democracies and to elaborate on what I hoped to accomplish as ambassador. Subsequently, I was contacted for background information by several reporters and invited to appear on several local TV programs. We repeated this event quarterly during my stay.

Almost immediately after our first luncheon, I was invited to appear on a very popular early morning television show called "Good Morning Barbados." Peter arrived to pick me up at 5:30 a.m. At the station, I was escorted to the dressing room for a professional touch up of my hair and makeup before facing the TV cameras. While I was sitting on the stool in the dressing room visiting with the staff, it became clear they were becoming more and more uncomfortable. It turned out they had no makeup appropriate for gray haired white women. We all laughed, agreed it was not a problem, and I pulled out my own little emergency makeup stash and all was well. I was on camera for about an hour. My hostess was well prepared with lots of good questions that gave me an opportunity to expound on the mutual benefits of a friendly relationship between our countries. There were some sensitive questions about Barbados/

U.S. relations, but they were "slow inside pitches" so I had plenty of time to respond appropriately. I appeared regularly thereafter on that widely viewed program. Clearly, those opportunities were part of the returns on investment from our media luncheons at the residence.

We wanted to reciprocate our lovely evening with British High Commissioner John White and his wife Judith, so as soon as we hired our chef, we invited them for dinner. They became our first dinner guests, and Chef Glen Walcott prepared an outstanding meal. He especially impressed John and Kay with the dessert of warm apple crisp and ice cream. By the end of the evening, the Whites felt like good friends and we anticipated spending time with them. John was a very senior diplomat with excellent insights.

Colleen Fretz, wife of Bob, had told us about the Brighton Farmer's Market and we expressed an interest in going. So she picked us up early on a Saturday morning and drove us to the market. That market was a place that we would enjoy visiting as many Saturday mornings as our schedule would allow. It was operated by Nick and Allyson Pyle. Nick was the *farmer* of the Farmer's Market. They lived on the grounds in a fabulous old colonial home that had been in his family for several hundred years. He and Allyson were both generous enough to offer us a tour, and then later on offered the same tour to visitors that wanted to get up early on a Saturday morning. Just off the small office room on the first floor was the hitching post, where for generations before, the horse would be delivered every morning so the plantation owner could ride out and look over the fields of sugar cane. Such history and tradition was valuable background. The market was always crowded, had beautiful vegetables, and served latte and cinnamon rolls. The Pyles laughingly named their morning brew "Pylebucks." After a visit to Iowa, we brought sweet corn seeds back with us. Nick grew the sweet corn and surprised us with some beautiful ears just before Christmas. So we surprised our family and friends by serving fresh, home grown corn on the cob for Christmas dinner our first year in Barbados.

One morning Kay looked at himself in the mirror and said to me "It's either a hair cut or a dog license." I was looking pretty shaggy as well, so once again I consulted with Peter and Rita. Peter told me about Donna Smith, a "mobile" hairdresser who would come to the residence. *Too good to be true.* Rita assured us she was a reliable person, and so for the rest of our stay we enjoyed the luxury of a hairdresser who came to us. She arrived early in the morning, about 7:30, gave both of us haircuts and was on her way. She had a thriving "mobile" business. A beautiful woman, she was a great walking advertisement for her own business. She also had a salon at the Fairmont Hotel and Resort, but she herself rarely worked there. And, she had "mobile" team members that would come to the residence to provide manicures and pedicures. *Is this heaven?*

Easter weekend was widely celebrated, and Doreen Weekes, the commercial officer at the embassy, invited us to attend Good Friday evening services at the historic cathedral in Bridgetown. Her husband was a leader in the music ministry there and a fine baritone singer. Thank goodness Peter dropped us off at the church courtyard; there was not room to turn around and the potential for running over graves in the cemetery was high. Clearly we were expected, because on our arrival we were escorted to the front of the cathedral by the bishop, who then formally welcomed us from the pulpit. The music was fabulous. The organ prelude included several Easter compositions by J.S. Bach; an accomplished vocal group accompanied by a fine small orchestra featuring a world-class young trumpeter performed the Bach B Minor Mass. I must admit this seasonal and timeless classical music came as a bit of a surprise in this Caribbean setting. But the musicians were so talented they would have been accepted and appreciated in any service anywhere in the world. Right after the prelude, during one of the hymns sung by the congregation, a true Caribbean moment occurred. The music apparently woke the doves in the rafters and they flew among the rafters, contributing their own sounds to the music. The congregation seemed to accept this as entirely appropriate. The cathedral was a large impressive building of gothic architecture dating to the 1500s. Gravestones in the churchyard dated back to the early 1600s.

A few short steps away from the cathedral grounds stood a perfectly restored Jewish synagogue, built for use as a temple by a group of Portuguese Jews who arrived in Barbados several hundred years ago while fleeing religious persecution in Brazil. The building had been empty and neglected for many years until Paul Altman undertook the renovation of both the synagogue and the graveyard surrounding it. Today, it stands as a testimony to the faith of those settlers and the vision of Mr. Altman; it is a sacred place for worship and visitation again.

Every year, we held an Easter egg hunt for the children of embassy employees on the residence lawn. We were often lonely for our own family so we looked forward to this gathering each year. What fun! A committee of embassy family members would arrive early to hide the eggs. They divided the lawn into three areas and the children, about 60 in all, were divided by age for the search. Another committee provided refreshments, and Chef Glen provided several large chocolate cakes as well. The cakes disappeared before the search for eggs even began. I cut and served cake while the gunny's wife handed out the traditional little yellow marshmallow chickens called Peeps. They are really awful and on no one's nutrition list—but the kids all loved them. Leo Voytko, the administrative officer, proved himself a real sport and donned an Easter Bunny outfit, then sat patiently for many, many photos. He and Consul General Bob Fretz made an unforgettable entrance. Bob dressed as Donald Duck and drove his wife's BMW convertible with the top down around to the backyard of the residence, with Leo as the Easter Bunny sitting beside him. The children went wild!

The gunnery sergeant's (head of our Marine battalion) family included adorable four-year-old twin girls. One little girl spent the morning dipping water from the fountain and pouring it down the front of her dress, while her sister fell in love with the Easter Bunny and insisted on appearing in every picture. She was crushed when it was time for him to leave. A good time was had by all.

On Easter Sunday, we made brunch reservations at Sandy Lane, an extravagant treat to be sure.

But first, we were scheduled to attend Easter service at the Holetown Methodist Church, the oldest church on Barbados, located at the bottom of the hill near the residence. We could drive ourselves there and on to brunch so Peter could enjoy Easter Sunday at home. The service was scheduled to begin at 9 a.m. so it seemed there would be plenty of time to make our 12:30 brunch reservation. The church was a small stone building with shutters and lovely stained-glass windows, which were wide open to catch the breeze. We arrived early and chose a pew beside a window and under a fan. Directly in front of us sat a lovely older woman dressed magnificently in yellow dress, hat and gloves. After we were seated for a moment, she turned around and said to Kay, "The books are over yonder." "Thank you," he replied.

A few moments later, she turned again and repeated in a much louder voice, pointing to the book rack by the side door. "THE BOOKS ARE OVER YONDER!" This time we understood, and Kay went to get two books for us. The woman nodded and smiled. The old wooden pews were so close together, there was barely enough room for one's knees, let alone racks for hymnals. The books themselves were quite small and contained only the words to the songs, no music. Many of the hymns were authored by John Wesley himself . I wondered how long these books had been in use, but there was no notation.

Still relative newcomers at that point, we were not yet widely recognized, especially since there were many British tourists in attendance. It was a wonderful service, spontaneous and spiritually uplifting. But it lasted more than three hours. There was a sharing time and many people felt called upon to share their worries and their good news. Everyone sang "Happy Birthday" to the organist while choir members presented him with flowers. Even with many ceiling fans and the old-fashioned stained-glass windows wide open, the church really warmed up when it was filled with people. The fan behind the pulpit wasn't working. At one point the pastor prayed earnestly for someone with electrical skills to come forward and fix it. It was all so real, human, sincere, and heartfelt one could not help but be touched.

When communion began, about 11:45, like most of the tourists we left the church only to find our car completely blocked in. So we went across the street and enjoyed coffee at Flindts while we waited for church to be over and the other parishioners to leave. As people began to pour out the front doors, we returned to stand beside our car. People nodded and spoke as they passed by. Finally a gentleman came up to Kay and asked, "You'd like to move your car?" Kay replied "Yes, please," so the man organized the other drivers to move their cars to allow to us back out and drive away, arriving only *slightly* late for our 12:30 brunch reservation. At Sandy Lane, valet parkers were waiting for us. The assistant manager, whom we had met previously, greeted us at the door. Like everyone who came into the hotel, we were greeted with a tray of very cold cloths dipped in eucalyptus water and a large fruit punch. We were then escorted to our table on the beach. A small fan had been placed on the floor near our table for two. We ate for nearly three hours. The steel pan orchestra was playing, and it was by any measure, the most lavish, beautifully presented and delicious brunch buffet we have ever attended, before or since. All in a memorable beach setting. Brunch cost something over $100 U.S. apiece; the champagne was included and it was memorable.

A group of Marines arrived from the States to build a hangar for the C-26 airplanes the U.S. provided for use in drug-enforcement efforts. The Marines stayed in Barbados for several months while they completed the hangar. This was a great public diplomacy opportunity, and staff had arranged for full media attendance at opening the event to welcome the Marines to Barbados. When I went to the airport grounds to participate in the event, I received the full military treatment. The Marines were formed up and waiting for me. "Attention! Present Arms!" They stood at attention until I reached the podium. Then "At Ease." Their precision and respect was almost overwhelming. I was expected to deliver a few remarks, but it was very hot and they were all standing and had been standing for some time. In my remarks I simply told them how much I admire the Marines and appreciated their service around the world. I mentioned how valuable this hangar would be to the C-26 operation and thanked them for coming to Barbados to complete the project. And then I sat down. *Ten minutes max.* Did I mention it was hot? During the reception that followed, a number of the young men, who were already very sunburned and looked miserable in their fatigues and boots, said they had been warned I would speak for at least 25 minutes. Needless to say I received many compliments on my remarks from these youngsters. There was no doubt in my mind that my brevity was far more valued than my content. Lesson learned.

Sir Harold St. John, well-loved and respected former Prime Minister of Barbados, died, and I was to attend my first state funeral, representing the U.S. government. I knew the black suit and the black hat were de rigueur. I felt I was a little too somber, so in the car on the way to the funeral I was pinning a deep red scarf on my hat. Peter looked back and said politely, "Madam

Ambassador, were you planning to wear that scarf?" I said, "Well yes, I was thinking about it." He responded, "Well, it will certainly make you outstanding." Enough said. The scarf remained in the car.

Bless Peter's heart; once again he gave good advice. The next day the papers included a picture and a stinging critique of the costume of an unfortunate government minister who had worn a light-blue suit and matching hat.

At this service, there was no chance to choose the seat by the window or the fan. The members of the Diplomatic Corps were formally escorted down the aisle of the church to seats that had been assigned according to length of service on the island. The service was a very formal Church of England liturgy, and all the priests wore very colorful vestments, including one with a full-length leopard skin vestment and hat. Did I mention it was HOT? With beautiful music and many comforting words, it was a lovely service for a man who was obviously considered one of Barbado's democratic heroes.

The junior officers at the embassy were an outstanding group who had worked extremely long and hard through the credential presentation rush. Many of them would be moving on at various times during the late spring and summer months as their Barbados tour concludes. They were bright and articulate, had unique and fascinating backgrounds, fun spouses and friends, and a real desire to serve their country. They also adapted quickly to new processes, were willing to offer their ideas, help improve productivity and to work as long and as hard as needed to get a job done. Kay and I decided to express our appreciation by entertaining them at a reception at the CMR. These young officers were thrilled to be invited and clearly enjoyed themselves. Later that evening I was told "Thank you for not being a 10 to 2 ambassador. At first we hoped you would just not get involved, but we're so glad you did." It took a moment for me to figure out what that 10 to 2 meant. I really appreciated the comment and responded, "Thanks. I'm just not capable of that kind of effort." The evening experience was a thank you for some very good work, but also an important part of coaching and mentoring. And, it was really fun.

Holders Festival is an annual month-long cultural event presented in an awesome natural setting on the grounds of the hosts of the festival, the Kidd family. It featured excellent professional musicians and actors who performed on various evenings throughout the month. We were told Pavarotti presented a concert several years previous and it was an outstanding event. We also learned that concert was very costly; the festival was still in debt. Events are held out of doors, with the huge trees behind the stages backlit so the audience had the feeling of depth and beauty. It was by far the loveliest, most intimate outdoor amphitheater we had ever seen. Every seat had an excellent view. During every performance, there is an hour-long intermission for supper.

During intermissions, spectators opened their very elegant picnic baskets and had very elegant parties on the lawn. Champagne flowed and performers mingled with the audience.

As a part of the Holders Festival, and through the efforts of our public affairs officer, we were able to sponsor an American pianist for one of the evening performances. Since the price to attend a concert was prohibitive for many families in Barbados, we asked music teachers to identify gifted students and invited a number of them to attend his performance. This was a win-win-win public diplomacy event. During intermission, we sponsored a reception for the students. The artist attended the reception, signed autographs for them and their chaperoning teachers, and discussed the demands of being a professional musician, the hours of practice and the rigors of travelling to perform. The students and their teachers were obviously greatly impressed. Next day, both newspapers featured articles with many pictures of the pianist and the students, so it was a public relations success as well.

We received an invitation to attend a polo match, the entertainment of choice on Sunday afternoons during "the season," meaning the winter months. During our time in Barbados, the sport grew from two polo fields to four, each one grander than the other, with elegant club houses, people beautifully dressed and exciting sport with beautiful horses. On this Sunday afternoon, Peter drove us directly to the club house with flags flying on the car. A parking place had been reserved for us. Our host was Mr. Melville, Chairman of the Polo Board, who greeted us and escorted us to our seats in the front row in the grassy area bordering the field. There were a few rose bushes and plantings in front of us; otherwise we were virtually on the field. Kay is allergic to horses so we were not sure how long he would last without watering eyes, sneezing and wheezing. He declined to join the crowd who go out in the grass to "stomp the divots" between chukkas, but otherwise got along fine. We enjoyed all three chukkas of all three matches. The final match of the afternoon was between two family teams. One of family members is a well known European fashion model. She was very tall, pencil thin and was dressed in jeans and boots with a sheer white blouse carelessly unbuttoned. I thought she looked stunning. While I was out stomping the divots, Kay was having refreshments and visiting with other spectators when he overheard a conversation behind him. Several women made note of the model's outfit and appearance. One asked "Which is the model?" Another replied "Can't you tell? The one with no tits!" Kay carefully avoided turning around to see who was carrying on this interesting conversation. He told me that although several comments occurred to him, he felt none of them would be "diplomatic." And then he said "See, that charm school really worked."

Before we arrived, Bonita had befriended the captain and crew of a catamaran called "Cool Runnings." They provided day-long cruises with excellent food and drink, and included several stops to snorkel with the fish and sea turtles. As with all her recommendations, this one was a winner. From our very first guests we got such rave reviews that we took nearly every group of visitors on the cruise. You just can't beat a relaxing day on the water, enjoying great food and rum punches while visiting with friends and family.

One Saturday during the Rosonkes' visit, backup driver Tony Cox drove us to the Cool Runnings dock. The armored car was a bit crowded with our guests, but we made it work. When it was time for our departure, Tony was waiting at the appointed place, but for some unknown reason, when it came time for the trip home, the door locking mechanism would only open the driver's door. While Tony desperately tried everything to unlock the other doors, we were standing on Main Street in Bridgetown in our swimsuits. Bonita came by and was horrified. The American ambassador was standing on the public street so she attempted to help. By this time, we had attracted quite a crowd, all making suggestions. Finally, we decided we would just all climb in through the driver's door. So we all crawled into the car through the driver's door, climbing over the front seat and into the back seat. We performed this feat on the main thoroughfare in Bridgetown in front of many witnesses. This struck us all so funny that on the way home we laughed till the tears flowed. Poor Tony was horribly embarrassed. It was a very good thing we were casually dressed. Performing that feat in business clothes would be really embarrassing, if not impossible. Thankfully our adventure did not make the papers.

We attended a reception given for the visiting British cricket team, hosted by British High Commissioner John and his wife Judith White. The party was held in that gorgeous garden party at their residence. A beautiful occasion with lots of people, including the members of both the West Indies and the British cricket teams. This would be similar to entertaining NFL or NBA stars in the U.S. Gorgeous young athletes. People were in awe of these young players—and IT WAS HOT. But good news. Kay met a number of potential golfing partners and agreed to become part of a regular Saturday morning golf group. However, the next afternoon, the British team won the match handily much to the consternation of the entire island.

Another interesting invitation, this time for cocktails on a French naval ship. Peter warned me not to wear high heeled sandals because I would be going up the gangplank and it was *not* a stairway. This was an official event so the flags were on the car, and Peter drove on the dock directly to the foot of the gangplank. We made it safely up the gangplank to be greeted by the Captain and the bosun with his whistle. We were formally "piped" on board and escorted through a double row of crew members in full dress white uniforms, all standing at attention and saluting. Thankfully, I had not disgraced myself on the way up the gangplank since there was such a large audience at the top. This was a lovely event and I had an agenda that included visiting with a number of the other guests. Since the crews of these ships include members from several different countries, our military folk had asked me to make some connections for them. I needed to work the room. Did I mention it was hot? The crew members seemed to be extremely young as they passed by serving drinks from their trays. I could see there was no ice in anything so I decided to have water. Pointing to a glass, I asked one of the servers "Is this water?" He smiled and nodded, so I picked up the tumbler and took a big drink. It was warm gin; straight, no mixer. I had a huge need to dash to the side of the ship and spit. But that would have been far too memorable an act for a U.S. ambassador. So I found a place to put the glass down while I tried to remember the French word for water. None of the waiters spoke English. I was finally successful, drank almost the whole glass and asked for another.

Meantime, Kay asked an officer "Where is the head?" thinking he was using the proper nautical term. The young officer responded "Let me escort you to the restroom sir." So much for his nautical jargon. Anyway, he learned it was air conditioned on the inside of the ship. He said he almost didn't come out again until it was time to go. H.C. John White had given more great advice. He told us to stay to the end of the evening, because the French would bring out fine Champagne and wonderful pastries. And they did. A buffet table covered with a white linen cloth was carried on deck. This was followed by a parade of young crew members with huge silver platters covered with beautifully prepared French pastries. Much to Kay's delight, one of the selections was his all time favorite dessert, chocolate éclairs. He said they were equal to his mothers. The crew members then returned with bottles of fine champagne and trays of crystal flutes. Excellent well chilled French Champagne was poured. Many toasts followed; it became obvious some folks had no problem drinking warm gin or whatever. Each toast seemed to be longer and more effusive than the one before. When it was time to leave, we sought out the Captain to make our farewells and thank him. We learned that if we're "piped on" we must be "piped off" as well. So the lines formed, the salutes took place, the farewell whistle was sounded and I managed the precarious trip back down the gangplank without incident.

Fourth of July celebrations are big events at Embassies around the world. Bridgetown was no exception. While planning for our first party, I was asked for "Iowa ideas." I suggested having the Police Band play patriotic marches, famous ones by John Philip Sousa and Karl King. And I mentioned that at some celebrations in Iowa, a whole pig is roasted on a spit over hot coals. Both ideas were met with enthusiasm by the committee. The first year celebration was terrific. Almost 500 of our closest new friends filled the grounds of the residence, the

Police Band played and the caterer had learned to roast a pig on a spit. Kay was a band director in a previous life and knew what was needed. He purchased band arrangements of some of the most famous marches and presented them to the conductor of the band. So the band not only played Sousa marches, they also played marches by Iowa's own band master, Karl King.

Our first Independence Day celebration was a great success, so a year later, the invitation for the second one was in great demand, a really "hot" ticket. The committee was challenged to make it even better. After our dear friends from New York, Drs. Les and Barbara Omatani had visited us, they presented me with my very own steel pan drum as a farewell gift. I loved playing it, and so I decided I would teach myself to play the Barbados National Anthem and God Bless America. It was difficult, because the steel pan scale bears no resemblance to any other musical instrument. Anyway, playing by ear, I practiced in the living room of the residence. We searched for music to the national anthem of Barbados and discovered there was no manuscript, at least we couldn't locate one, so I needed to listen carefully. As I was practicing, Rita and Glen would come into the room from time to time to correct my mistakes. By singing the correct version for me they helped to be sure I had it right. At times, their efforts to teach me the tune could have been terrific material for one of the world's funniest videos. Anyway, the night finally arrived and I was as nervous as I have ever been about a performance. For heaven's sakes, everyone KNOWS these songs. If I make a mistake, everyone will KNOW I made a mistake. Once again, Kay was the emcee, and he introduced me by saying "The ambassador has prepared a surprise for you." My knees were knocking so I simply said "To honor Barbados," and began to play. *It was one of those unforgettable moments.* The whole crowd went silent. No one coughed or sneezed, and about half way through, people began to hum along; not singing, just quiet humming. I was so moved, I was nearly in tears. At the end of the Barbados anthem, there was absolute silence. I said "To honor America," and began to play God Bless America. Again, stillness and silence from the crowd, until the Americans present very softly began to hum along. By this time I was not very successful at holding back tears—yet wishing I could prolong the moment; one I will never forget. That performance turned out to be a watershed moment in my stay in Barbados. I had no idea that people would be so appreciative and I would feel so much affection from then on. The fact that I took the time and effort to learn to play their anthem on their instrument was so meaningful. I have long believed in the power of music to bridge cultures and to build friendships. But the after effects of that night reinforced my belief many times over.

The Marine Ball Ceremony occurs annually around the world as a celebration of the founding of The Corps. Wherever a group of Marines are serving, no matter how small, they gather in November to honor their fallen comrades.

It might be a simple gathering or a formal and elegant Marine Ball, but every one of them is a very special event.

Whatever the venue, every Marine present wears their dress blue uniform and participates in a solemn and traditional ceremony of remembrance for the fallen comrades. When the guests arrive they see a small table in a place of honor, set for one. This symbolizes remembering the Marine who is absent because he/she has fallen defending our country. The table is beautifully and formally set, with white linen tablecloth, white china, silver and glassware, and decorated with a crystal bud vase holding a single red rose. A pair of white gloves, like those worn with the formal uniform on formal occasions, is draped over the plate.

The event begins with the presentation of the colors. The gunny and the ambassador welcomes the guests, and the gunny introduces the highest ranking Marine present. That Marine steps forward, asks everyone present, to stand. He then moves to stand near the symbolic table while the commemoration message is read aloud. There is absolute silence.

After the reading is completed, the gunny escorts the ambassador, followed by the oldest Marine present and the youngest Marine present to the table where the cake honoring the Marine Corps birthday is displayed.

The ambassador cuts the first piece and presents it to the highest ranking Marine present. He/she takes the plate and presents it to the youngest Marine, who serves the plate to the oldest Marine present. After the oldest Marine has partaken, he offers the plate to the youngest Marine, who partakes as well. Cake is then served to all and the birthday celebration begins.

Each time I was honored to participate in this ceremony, it was a deeply emotional experience. I learned to love and appreciate each of the young men and women Marines who served in Bridgetown. The poignant reminder of the fallen comrade and the service of the cake from the oldest to the youngest is a beautiful and symbolic reminder that these men and women have chosen to risk their lives to assure the continuance of liberty in our country. Their pride in the Corps and their pride in their comrades is a beautiful thing.

So much happened and so quickly, I am thankful I found the time to keep a journal. Without my scribbling, some memories would surely be blurred or lost.

At some point, I began to realize there was the steady accumulation of information coming my way on the state of affairs before I arrived. I did not ask questions, I just waited and watched and worked, and as trust developed, information began to make its way to me. As the weeks passed and the house staff and security officers began to trust both Kay and me, they became more forthcoming. There was no point, nothing to be gained, in going into detail. Suffices to say as more thorough informal conversations, through some carefully worded and polite references, we began to understand that some previous ambassadors had not been perceived as productive or helpful. Some had clearly been appointed as a political thank you, with little expectation of substance, spending their time making public appearances and attending social events. In politics, they are called "ribbon-cutters." My immediate predecessor had formed connections, both Bajan and international and some of those connections raised both suspicion and caution. Not the reputation we would hope for our country's representative abroad.

These carefully worded conversations clarified why that congressional staffer asked me if I was prepared to clean up the mess down there, why the DCM said at the end of our first meeting with a sigh of relief "We're going to get along really well," and why the president said "Mary, we need some of that good Midwest common sense down there."

It took several months time before there was enough trust established that I began to learn some of the details of the "mess" left behind. And even then, it was through back-door channels. To protect people's privacy, I will say no more. My predecessor apparently made a series of dubious choices that had harmful repercussions in Barbados society as well as in several agencies of the U.S. government. I don't know how to put it any more "Iowa nice" than that. Because of that, early on we dealt with a subtle attitude of suspicion from everyone from embassy employees, to government officials, to the house staff. Everyone wondered what kind of persons the U.S. was sending them this time. As we reached out to make friends, and people discovered that Kay and I had their best interests in mind, and intended to work hard, they were overwhelmingly open and friendly. Our house staff bent over backwards to do anything for us. They became resources; providing information and cultural advice that was immensely useful. They helped us to avoid many cultural gaffes that would have been embarrassing to us and our country and slowed our progress. We were never allowed to open a door, wash a dish, even fold our own laundry.

And so it became clear to me that in addition to our many official duties, it would also be part of our job to mend damaged relationships and rehabilitate the impression of U.S. ambassadors, and by extension, their impression of America. Happily, it did not take long for the warm, hospitable people of the islands to accept us at face value and when they could see we were truly honored and just delighted to be there to serve our country, to help our hosts build up their countries and to accomplish mutual goals, we were accepted unconditionally.

In this chapter, I have tried to describe the hectic schedule of wonderfully diverse events that began on arrival and continued throughout our stay. We entertained adult guests from home nearly every week from mid October to late May, and then families after school dismissed for the summer. We enjoyed hosting receptions for groups of people from colleges like St. Olaf or Wartburg, or the University of South Carolina, as well as groups who were traveling the Caribbean on cruises. We learned to love the diplomatic life that was crowded with work and activities, fast paced, and filled with opportunities to make a positive difference for our country and for the wonderful people of these seven lovely islands. Each of our visitors, whether official or family and friends, were special to us, and enhanced our experience. We were so fortunate that our families were able to make so many visits. Missing them would have been nearly intolerable if we didn't get to see them more often than just when we were able to make home visits. Thankfully our house staff enjoyed them as well. This was extremely important because visitors added much to the work of the household, and staff did *all* the work. Each day we were humbled and thankful we could share in this unique life's experience.

CHAPTER SIX

THE NICE LADY FROM IOWA INSISTS — NO MORE LONE RANGERS

Every embassy around the world has a country team. That team has the *potential* to be an effective and powerful front line for diplomacy. The highest-ranking officers of the multiple agencies represented at the embassy, all of whom report to the ambassador, form the members of the team. Or so I'd been told. In Bridgetown, these would be the resident heads of the Department of State (DOS), the Drug Enforcement Agency (DEA), the Federal Bureau of Investigation (FBI), the Internal Revenue Service (IRS), the Military Liaison Office (MLO), the Office of U.S. Foreign Disaster Assistance (OFDA), the Consul General for the Region, the Regional Security Officers (RSO), United States Agency for International Development (USAID) and other non-resident groups who worked in the region, such as the Department of Homeland Security (DHS). Team members were the people engaged in leading the missions of their bureaus, or agencies or departments. When the team worked together, the potential to advance a democratic agenda, achieve foreign policy goals, and influence hearts and minds all over the world is huge. Few Americans are even aware of the existence of a country team, but team members work tirelessly on behalf of every American to promote the cause of peace, prosperity and democracy on a global scale.

Or so it could go when the country team works together. But the reality I discovered in Barbados was much different. Individually, many of the members of my country team had the potential to be superstars, and there were individual victories and achievements to be celebrated. But collectively, we were nowhere near reaching our potential, not only for the success of their individual missions in Barbados but by extension, furthering the foreign policy goals for the good of the people of America. The country team members I encountered when I arrived were a group of lone rangers, interested in carrying out their own individual missions. They reported first to Washington, and second—a distant second—to the ambassador. And why not? None of them expected the ambassador or their fellow team members to have any desire to forward their agendas, so none of them saw any reason to assist anyone else. As a matter of fact, I believe many of them thought the ambassador was more likely to be a detriment or hindrance rather than a help, and so were wary of sharing information or even suggesting ways to work together. Perhaps privately, they even hoped the ambassador would not be too engaged in the day to day activities of the embassy.

I'm not blaming anyone; to the contrary, this is the status quo at work. Adding to the wariness, I learned that some previous ambassadors showed up for meetings only to be updated. Too often, the examples of disinterest and poor leadership, along with a lack of desire to lead change or to foster team-building, only increased the attitudes of noncooperation among the country team members and ultimately among the agencies they represented. Why risk sharing hard won individual relationships, results and achievements when you could be relatively successful on your own? The attitude of the country team members was a microcosm of the attitudes in Washington that I witnessed there, where agencies operated in their independent silos on carefully protected turf and were loathe to share information with one another, much less collaborating. *Our federal government suffers from a huge disconnect,* both, inter and intra agency, and that makes the work of embassy teams more difficult by a multiple of at least 100. When there is no incentive to work across agency lines, or even across the isolated "silos" within agencies, persons in leadership roles are unable or unwilling to depart from the way things have always been done. In fact, *every* incentive encourages people to maintain the status quo, to do things the "way we've always done them." If there is any collaborative work, it comes from individual country teams around the world. This attitude reflects a computer generated phrase on most elementary school report cards, "Does not play well with others," and any fifth grader knows that is not a good thing.

After mulling over this problem for a while, I decided to visit with Marcia to see if she would have problems or if she had concerns about making radical changes in the meeting format of the country team. She seemed relieved that I was willing to tackle the issue. Apparently the fact that most attendees thought meetings were a waste of time was a regular topic of water cooler conversations, but no one was willing to speak up publicly.

So, I had a big problem on my hands, and one that needed to be fixed yesterday if we were to have any hope of getting meaningful work accomplished. So, at the next Tuesday meeting of the group, I told them what the president's directive/goal for me was; to *maintain stable democracies.* That was my goal, so that was my expectation that would drive all of our Embassy efforts. Then, without preamble, I asked each of them point-blank what they did personally and professionally to support that embassy mission. They were shocked by the question, and no one felt they could give a satisfactory answer.

"OK," I said, "let's adjourn for today. By our next meeting, be prepared to discuss how each of your individual agendas supports the overall embassy mission. If anyone has a problem with what that is, I'll be happy to stay behind and discuss it with you right now, or you can make an appointment to visit with me."

Thirty stunned people left the room in silence.

That afternoon, via email, I instituted immediate changes in format for our meetings so that we could begin to work more efficiently. Changes that put the emphasis on collaboration.

Beginning immediately, information and announcements that I or other team members needed to know should be submitted to Bonita via email. She would assimilate them and distribute them via email before the meetings. The current meeting practice was taking several hours going around the table so that every person had the opportunity to share everything they had been doing the week before. The email distribution would eliminate that practice, making room for substantive issues that would benefit from a more in depth discussion. I would be submitting some issues myself, but I expected that others would do so as well. These substantive issues would henceforth make up our meeting agenda. When team members submitted items to be placed on our agenda, they should include very brief salient background information and an estimation of the time needed for discussion. The person submitting the item would be asked to lead discussion.

I assured them this was not an attempt to eliminate discussion; it was an attempt to focus the discussion on important issues. For the first few weeks, Marcia's or my issues were the only items on our agenda. But as discussion became fruitful, people became more comfortable sharing real information. It took a awhile for agenda items to be forthcoming. These changes in format caused our meetings to go from three hours per week to one hour per week. This alone earned me hero status among some members. It also ensured that each member was aware of their opportunity to play an active role, both in setting the agenda and collaborating on issues.

I scheduled regular weekly meetings with each leader. These meetings gave me the opportunity to listen to what each member felt they needed to accomplish on behalf of their agency, but it also gave me the opportunity to emphasize the fact that the changes in meeting format were not intended to stifle discussion. Rather, they were intended to provide time for fruitful and strategic consideration of key issues. I shared my belief that meetings lasting longer than one hour became counterproductive. I looked for issues that would benefit from group discussion and encouraged them to submit them to the agenda. I also took every opportunity to ask what I could do to further the achievement of their individual goals and mission.

At that next meeting every individual rose to the task, as I suspected (and hoped) they would. Every member was able to describe his or her individual mission and explain how their individual efforts supported the collective Embassy mission of maintaining stable democracies. I think some were surprised to learn what others were attempting to accomplish, and this knowledge increased their appreciation for the work being done by their colleagues. And with a common goal, we began to see ourselves as part of a team. Each team member had developed a variety of relationships and networks and information sharing from all these various perspectives was remarkably useful to all. We started to see ourselves in a win-win situation, individual agenda items could be discussed with appropriate actions agreed to. We began to hear comments like"I can help with that" or "Have you thought about contacting _____."

No matter what the workplace, time is a valuable commodity for a group of leaders who have much to accomplish. This country team, which covered seven different nations, was no exception. At each individual meeting, I received immediate and positive feedback on the changes and my expectations. Not surprisingly, those who had complained the loudest about unproductive and boring meetings were the same people who had the most difficulty remembering to submit their accomplishments and announcements and who tried to continue their practice of dominating discussion in the new format. Some things seem to be the same the world over. Still, the changes made an immediate and positive difference. The team began to function differently; we were creating an opportunity to live up to our potential.

I believe that the members of country teams in every embassy around the world not only form the front lines of our diplomatic efforts, but they have the potential to advance the democratic agenda, enhance the national security agenda, achieve foreign policy goals, influence hearts and minds and serve the United States in new and better ways, producing superior results we cannot even imagine.

My brief weekly meetings with each team leader-fifteen to thirty minutes, sometimes standing up-helped me to understand their issues and exponentially increased my understanding of my colleagues and their missions.

My first meeting was with Consul General Bob Fretz. First order of business, I assured him I was not going to be in the business of interfering in the process of granting visas. During Charm School I had been told that many ambassadors felt this was their prerogative. Even though it was already obvious I was going to get lots of requests to intervene, I simply did not understand the rules, and I had neither the time nor the desire to learn them. I would refer all requests to him. He was an outstanding guy who had demonstrated himself capable of improving the performance and productivity of his area when I arrived. Marcia had told me he arrived to chaos. The embassy was making the newspapers almost every day, mostly due to some really egregious incident with a visa applicant. *We were losing passports for heaven's sake.* We either wouldn't, or couldn't, respond to questions about the progress of applications. After 9/11 all applicants were required to fly to Barbados because they were required to appear in person. In our area of the world, this meant that people would be required to purchase a plane ticket, fly to Barbados, only to wait in line for an entire day and be told to come back tomorrow. Then if they could afford one, they would get a hotel room and spend the night. The application itself at that time cost $100 U.S., whether or not the visa was granted. This constituted a huge investment just to apply. Bob had over 20 years experience in the consular business, spoke seven or eight languages fluently. He knew his stuff. Working with newly assigned and very bright officers, and the locally employed consulate staff, he improved the customer service aspect of his business about 110% in a few short months. I called him a very successful turnaround manager. Thankfully, by the time I met with the media, we were no longer making the papers several days a week with horror stories about the treatment of visa applicants. Newly instituted online appointment processes were underway.
The process improvement began making appointments for off-island applicants in the morning and Bajans in the afternoon. This simple change went a long way to easing the problems. The morning applicants who were granted visas could often pick up their completed paperwork and return home that afternoon. The lines were short, usually including only those people who had not made appointments. To be sure, we had some people who did not know of the online appointment process and just showed up, but the volume was manageable. Thanks to Marcia and Bob, and the whole consular team, we had created an exemplary visa line. Complaints dropped nearly to zero, and the newspapers provided some very complimentary coverage about the changes.

There was still some resentment among applicants that they were required to pay the application fee whether they received their visa or not. This had been the topic of a public discussion in parliament. The fee covered the costs for managing the process, which became much more complex after 9/11. Still, many of the applicants are very poor people and they pay the application fee, purchase a plane ticket to come and stand in line, even sometimes stay overnight. That is a big investment for a visa to the U.S. And yet the appetite for visas remains *huge*, not only in the Caribbean but around the world. This appetite is very clear evidence that America is still viewed as the land of opportunity. Sometimes it seemed that people who want to come here and seek that opportunity perhaps have a greater appreciation for that opportunity than some of us who are blessed by birth to live here and are able to take their liberty and quality of life for granted.

During my one-on-one meetings, nearly every team member expressed interest in learning more about leadership and developing their individual leadership skills. They all expressed appreciation for the more satisfying results from the country team.

As a result of these meetings, I began a separate series of leadership training sessions, purely voluntary, for anyone who wanted to attend. These sessions allowed me to engage in something I loved doing; coaching and mentoring. The sessions were so in demand, I agreed to repeat sessions for people who traveled. Few of the country team members had ever experienced leadership training, and they seemed to be hungry for it. Faster than I hoped, or would have thought possible, we were functioning as a cohesive group with common goals, and we got incredible work done.

Really fun stuff!

In a few weeks, I was prepared to lead the discussion on how we were going to get a return on the investments we made while presenting credentials. Team members actually admitted there was virtually no expectation that we would actually achieve our six week goal, so getting a return on that investment of time and financial resources was new thinking. Still, everyone had participated in the preparation, and there was a shared sense of accomplishment when those goals were met. I was told, rather sheepishly by some, that everyone had agreed it was a great plan, but no one expected it to be accomplished.

The strategic question still loomed. How would we get a return on the investment of the time and money spent on the credential presentation process? How can the learning from all this listening be applied to various segments of the societies. The learning curve had already been steep and there was much more to understand. To move my own learning curve along,

I planned to make a strategic plan for each of our islands, beginning with their environmental analysis. This would be my method of determining current conditions regarding those things necessary in a stable democracy:

- stable governments with free and fair elections;

- an understanding of the revenue streams;

- some public health infrastructure (at least clean water and health care providers and facilities);

- universal public education;

- a functioning legal system with competent law enforcement;

- transparent and honest regulation in order to attract foreign capital; and

- respect for human rights.

Since I could not begin to complete these plans without input, everyone went to work on providing insight from their perspective. Taken together, their data and ideas would provide the base of information that would enable us to set goals for working with each country.

And just in time, too. We were about to have a Level 1 diplomatic situation on our hands.

President Bush with my granddaughter Kelsey
at a campaign event in Des Moines

White House Christmas Party "Merry Christmas, Mrs. Bush"

Me and Karl Rove
"Shall I call you Ambassador yet?"

The "A" Team
Becky Beach, me, Kaye Lozier

Laura Bush and me

Secretary of State Colin Powell administers the oath of office

My acceptance speech

Kent, Kim, Kay, me, Secretary Powell, Krista, Scott,
Kay's sister Nancy, and her husband and Dr. Mike Graham

"You're on my team sister!"

Leaving Iowa in January

Beautiful sunset from our backyard

Bonita Estes

Our backyard at the residence

Ricardo, Glen, Rita, and Norma—
our family in Barbados

My driver and friend—Peter Jean Bapliste

First dinner for two

First Saturday at the Round House— not a painting behind us

Marcia Bernicat and John Regan

Road signs in Barbados

Ahhh, Kay's first swim in
the backyard pool

Gardener David at work
picking coconuts

Me in my hat

Our first green monkey sighting

Presenting credentials to Barbados' Governor
General Clifford Husbands

Reviewing the troops on National Days

Carib country in Dominica

The women of the Coal Pot
Soup Factory in Dominica

Me and Peace Corps
Volunteers in St. Lucia

Kay's "plastic" Toyota

Yes, steering wheel is
on the wrong side

Kay, me, Dick and
Mary Ann Rosonkes at Flindts

Governor General of St. Lucia
Dame Pearlette Louisy and me

Cousins reunion -
Caryn Hastings, Phil Lotz,
Robert Hastings, Marge Lotz, and Kay

Ribbon cutting as we reopen a Peace Corps Office in St. Kitts

The Easter Bunny at the residence

Prime Minister Arthur—unplanned
speaker at our welcome reception

Myself, Governor General
of Antigua and Juliet Ryder

Me and Dame Billie

Touches of home

Cool Runnings -
great catamaran fun for all

Kay and I at our front gate

With Kim and the granddaughters
during their first visit to Barbados

Christmas on Cool Runnings—
Captain Robert and Kent, Kim, Kelsey,
Kallen, Karsen, and Kennedy

Granddaughter Kennedy with the turtles

Ivan's terrible destruction

Consul General Bob Fretz

Secretary Powell's visit to Grenada

Kay, Scott, Krista, and me—Never enough family visits

Presenting music to the leader
of the police band

Barbados Royal Police Force Band
performing in our backyard gazebo

Marcia, Attorney General Mia Mottley, and me on Independence Day

High Commissioner White, Prime Minister
Tony Blair, me, Prime Minister Arther, and
Kay at reception honoring Mr. Blair

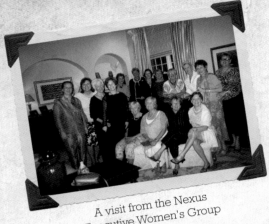

A visit from the Nexus
Executive Women's Group

Thanksgiving dinner
with the Marines

Friends and family gather
for Christmas Dinner

Scott and Krista—New Year's Eve
on the beach with fireworks

Kay volunteering at
Candlelight and Carols

Part of the crowd at
Candlelight and Carols

My steel pan solo

The Hartman family visits for July 4th celebrations

S.I.R. Harlie Smith, S.I.R. Kay Kramer,
Kent and Kim Kramer, and me
with DCM Meg Gilroy

Reading to children at story hour

Moonlight over our patio

Farewell picture at the front door

Marines presenting the colors

Kay and me at our retirement ceremony

CHAPTER SEVEN

CARICOM, CULTURES, CONFRONTATIONS AND ARISTIDE

CARICOM, the acronym for Caribbean Community (originally the Caribbean Community and Common Market), is the loose association of fifteen Caribbean states. Emphasis on "loose." Although these islands are all famous for sea, sun, and sand, they also have very different cultures and histories. Most Americans have a limited vision of the region of the carefully manicured glimpses seen through tourist advertising. They may have been on a cruise with several Caribbean ports of call and are vaguely aware of the pristine beaches but of the antiquity and poverty present in the islands. Both the seaport and airport facilities are specifically designed to appeal to tourists. So if the visit is limited to tourist experiences, each island presents remarkable similarities. This furthers the impression that the islands are identical septuplets.

This is hardly the case. Not only did I discover how different each island was, I learned that even in this age of the Internet and globalization, there's much less cross-pollination, so to speak, than you might imagine. Inter-island experience among native populations is amazingly limited. In fact, many island residents have never been away from the island on which they were born. Cost of travel is so prohibitive their children don't compete in sports from island to island, their artists are rarely hired to work on another island and family members rarely go to other islands to find work or to visit or vacation. Instead they seek visas to go to Canada, the U.S., or the United Kingdom.

There was no free flow of labor from island to island, since even fellow Caribbean laborers were considered "foreign" labor; they were not welcomed to seek jobs. Work permits were very difficult to obtain, even for other islanders. The most desired immigration visas are to the U.S. or the United Kingdom. Immigration visas among the islands of the Caribbean are rare. It's OK to visit your cousin, but not to stay and get a job.

Barbados had always been a British "colony" until achieving independence forty years ago. It is said that Barbados today is more British than Great Britain. Throughout their history, the other six islands of the Eastern Caribbean have all been subject to domination by the British, the Dutch, the French, or the Spanish, or several of the above. One can find well preserved old forts in each of these countries. Sometimes built by the French, sometimes by the British, sometimes the Spanish, at various times in history, these forts had different landlords. For example, on St. Kitts, two forts still exist. Of historic interest, one was built by the British at the top of the hill and one was built by the French, about half way down the same hill. Both overlook the harbor to protect against invasion from the sea. It makes one wonder what kind of battles were fought up and down that hill as armies tried to maintain their control of their forts and of the island. During World War II, the U.S. maintained a naval base on St. Lucia and an airport facility on Antigua.

After reading the history and learning about the demographics and the state of development of these small island economies, I began to wonder if any of them possessed an economy of scale large enough to individually support the infrastructure necessary for independence, i.e., respect for the rule of law. meaning competent law enforcement; free and fair elections, meaning there is an opposition party; public health provisions, including clean water and health care providers and facilities; economic development, requiring an infrastructure of roads and utilities, including dependable electricity; and public education, as a healthy democracy requires educated citizens to participate. Continual problems providing and maintaining these basic necessities put the country's leaders in the position of continual foreign fund raising. They travelled the world asking for money. One unfortunate strategy was the use of their vote in the U.N. General Assembly for leverage or trading stock.

Given their size and their internal revenue opportunities, I silently wondered if could they ever really be self sustaining. This was not a question to be asked out loud, but it provided food for thought as we studied these small economies and worked to build relationships with government leaders. Keep in mind there were two primary sources of island revenue. The first was tourism, and while they were blessed with the weather and the geography attractive to tourists, the industry is vulnerable to weather and the health of world economies, and requires an expensive infrastructure of hotels, restaurants and attractions. The second was remittances, the voluntary contributions sent to family members from relatives working out of the country—largely from the U.S. and the United Kingdom. Both sources were unpredictable and did not lend themselves to diversifying the economies.

Barbados was by far the most sophisticated and wealthy of our countries, with world class resorts and restaurants. Still, the grocery stores might be completely out of milk for days at a time. The meat counters might be empty for days running, and no one complained. Kind of a philosophical acceptance, "these things happen."

Tourism jobs are considered *very good* jobs in the Caribbean and were highly desired. The government agencies involved with the labor force were persistent and insistent on sending employees to U.S. resorts so they could learn to work in hotels and restaurants; exporting labor was a profitable business. I attended many meetings and responded to many requests to add to the temporary worker visa availability so that more people could come to the U.S. to work in the tourism industry in the Carolinas or the Florida/Georgia/Alabama corridor. If they got a visa to stay, so much the better because that meant remittances would begin coming to family members.

Coming from the Midwest, I had to keep reminding myself that these are all *island* nations; you just can't get in a car and drive from one island to another. This meant the individual members of CARICOM have been somewhat insulated and isolated from one another, leaving them cautious, even suspicious, certainly not trusting of each other. More trade among the islands and a freer labor flow has great potential for creating jobs and growing economies, so we tried to work around or through some of these decades-long differences and prejudices to find ways to create a more open market in the Caribbean.

Examples of our efforts include the collaboration between USAID and the University of the West Indies (UWI), a prestigious Caribbean university with campuses on several of the islands. Working together, we conducted a year-long training program to help leaders from the government and the business community to increase their trade negotiating skills. Training opportunities were provided for people from the government and from the legal profession to develop skills at drafting the legislation necessary for freer trade and movement of labor, especially skilled labor. This resulted in an ongoing work group at CARICOM headquarters that was extremely competent.

I have only small successes to report along these lines, and most of the success stories involved providing technical assistance to Caribbean companies in finding niche markets for their products in the U.S. or in other countries. One of those success stories involved the manufacture and sale of the solar water heater. A manufacturer in Barbados sold his solar water heaters throughout the region. Barbados is the second largest user and exporter of solar heating units in the world, second only to Israel. To his credit, the company president determined he could also manufacture them in St. Kitts and was in the process of opening a factory there. He would employ local workers and market to local people. A great example of business acumen! But he figured out how to be successful, not by exporting the water heaters to St. Kitts, but because the manufactured them there. It's a business success story, but it was not an example of furthering freer trade among the islands.

Earlier, I described my visit to the Coal Pot Soap Factory on Dominica. This small group of entrepreneurial women encountered manufacture and distribution problems of another kind. They manufacture wonderful soaps, oils and other cosmetic products. They accomplish this in a small cinder block building using an old bottled gas stove very similar to the one that was in my grandparents' kitchen on the farm in Iowa over 60 years ago. These young entrepreneurs are beautiful. If their lovely skin could become an example of the results of using their product, every woman in America would want to become a customer. The Peace Corps Volunteer that helped develop their business had long since gone. To their credit, they managed to keep the business profitable by making enough products to fulfill the orders that came to them. They supply soap products for the guest rooms at the Hotel Fort Young, and this business alone creates enough follow-up Internet orders to stretch their fulfillment capacity to the limit. But here's the hard part. Even though there was great opportunity to grow the business, they lacked knowledge and capital to expand their production capacity. Several of the cruise lines expressed interest in placing the Coal Pot products in their staterooms. The women very wisely saw they could not regularly fulfill large orders and were fearful they might lose the hotel as their regular customer if they were not able to maintain a regular supply. So they maintained their sales to the hotel and the Internet business it generated, but did not seek growth. This economic development issue was repeated all over the Caribbean. There were great ideas and opportunity, abundant natural raw materials and hard working entrepreneurial people who saw no way to grow. The concepts of expansion and capital formation were foreign. And while I understood and applauded their decision not to accept more orders than they knew they could fulfill within their current operation, the extent of their limitations was disappointing. Five jobs would remain five jobs in their village. No way to expand to even six jobs, let alone 15 or 20.

Another example. For generations, the banana industry had been the backbone of the economies of several of these islands. That industry is a good example of how globalization damaged small economies. It functioned very simply. Small farmers in Dominica and other islands would take their crops to the port once a week, receive cash for their bananas and in turn pay the people (mostly family members) who worked with them. The revenue generated supported much of the island population either directly or indirectly. American companies like Dole and Chiquita, as well as large European companies located in North Africa, expanded their fields and began trading large quantities of bananas on the world market. The economy of scale and efficiency of their operations in Central and South America made it impossible for small individual growers to compete, either in price or in quality. In addition, wages and the cost of living were much lower than in the small islands of the Caribbean. So the banana industry, the backbone of the island economies, failed. Today, the only market available is to the island grocer or selling the fruit as street vendors.

Since Dole and Chiquita were viewed as American companies, the U.S. was blamed for the failure of the industry. Dominicans saw no way of becoming competitive raising bananas simply because the topography, the limited size of the island and the lack of room to expand cultivation prevent increases in productivity or mass production. The government was nearly bankrupt, so no subsidy could even be considered. An agriculture problem indeed. Substitute crops that would have provided income for these farmers simply could not be found. Similar problems with similar consequences occured in St. Vincent and St. Lucia. Actually, a number of farmers in St. Vincent had turned to growing marijuana as their cash crop. And they did it very successfully. But that's another story.

A similar situation occurred in St. Kitts. The government subsidy of the sugar industry nearly bankrupted the country. Finally, there was no alternative but to stop growing and processing the sugar cane. This was a politically difficult and unpopular decision. For St. Kitts and Barbados, sugar cane growth and production had been the driving force of island agricultural societies for centuries. In fact, some people believed Americans owed them a debt of gratitude because nearly 300 years ago the British decided sugar cane was more valuable than the American "colonies" and so did not commit enough resources, thus allowing us to defeat the British and win our liberty. Truth or fiction? Hard to know, but it does emphasize how important the sugar cane industry was in the colonial world.

"Crop Over" occurs annually in Barbados. It is a week-long festival celebrating the completion of the sugar cane harvest. Harvesting sugar cane involves manually cutting the cane stalks using huge scythes for tools. This is hot, backbreaking physical labor. The King and Queen of Crop Over were selected and honored not for their beauty or talent, but for their skill and endurance in cutting cane. Because of small fields and rolling terrain, there was little opportunity for a mechanized harvest. As in the banana industry, the high cost of production compared to larger Third World nations with much lower labor costs raised the price of the raw sugar produced in the islands and made it non-competitive in the global marketplace. Barbados was somewhat more fortunate, in that the molasses used to make rum is a sugar by-product, and Barbados was a large producer, marketer and exporter of very excellent rum. In fact, Mount Gay is over 300 years old, one of the oldest rums produced in the world.

On St. Kitts, when they stopped growing cane, several thousand citizens were immediately unemployed. Worse, because their skills consisted solely of cutting cane, they were virtually unemployable. There was no other industry or activity in place that could employ them. The government announced they were stopping production a year in advance and sought training assistance so the workers could compete for other jobs, but WHAT other jobs?

There is one thing however, on which the Caribbean elected officials unite instantly and intractably. That one thing is regime change, and it precipitated one of the most eye-opening moments I experienced as an ambassador. It was a learning experience that would change my approach in several ways. The specific event I'm referring to is now infamous. There are multiple versions of the story, but I can tell you mine. In 2004, as the political situation in Haiti began to deteriorate and armed insurgents were nearing the presidential palace, a frightened President Jean-Bertrand Aristide reached out to the State Department for help. He contacted Secretary Powell through the U.S. ambassador to Haiti to request that the U.S. assist him in escaping his country. Secretary Powell agreed to provide assistance, and a U.S. plane was immediately dispatched to take Aristide to safety. In a matter of hours the rescue plane was in Haiti. It was clear that President Aristide, his wife and family, along with a few close associates, required an armed escort to the airport. The U.S. military liaison group from the embassy, along with Aristide's own security force, performed escort services. Within an hour after landing, Aristide, his wife and family, and a few close associates were onboard and airborne. Meanwhile, a search was underway for a country that would receive him. It soon became apparent that few countries were willing or able to provide hospitality, but eventually the Central African Republic agreed to provide asylum. After landing and learning of his whereabouts, Aristide objected to the destination, and accused the U.S. government, Secretary Powell in particular, of having him kidnapped so that America could replace him with our own choice of leader. Media reports of the circumstances were many, mostly inaccurate and focused on the escalating rhetoric coming from Aristide. The Caribbean was in a frenzy, and elected officials from most every island rushed to get on record with an opinion.

For example, my self-appointed "best friend," PM Ralph Gonsolves of St. Vincent, was seen on television the very next day and was widely quoted in the newspapers throughout the region criticizing Secretary Powell. He was dramatic, angry and very personal in his attack. When I called him to let him know how offensive his remarks were, he assured me he was misquoted. "I think the world of Colin," he told me. Not only had I seen him on television myself, but I found his use of first names and his patronizing tone extremely offensive, so it became a very brief and very chilly discussion that ended abruptly. My point was made but the damage was done. He called back the next day to see how "his sister from Iowa" was enjoying the Caribbean and issued a personal invitation for Kay and me to spend a long weekend with him and his wife in St. Vincent. *Not going to happen!*

Up until this point in my tenure, meetings with Barbados Foreign Minister Dame Billie Miller had been open and cordial, even though we had disagreed on some issues. My meeting with her regarding the Aristide situation was palpably different. She was defensive, a little hostile and clearly unwilling to listen to my, i.e. the U.S., explanation of events.

She was the current Chair of the CARICOM Organization of Foreign Ministers (COFCOR) at the time, and Washington was interested in knowing her position on the issue. At the time, she had not spoken publicly. Most people in Washington were surprised that she accepted the meeting, because in the months prior to my arrival a pattern had emerged. An official who wished to avoid face to face discussions over difficult issues would simply be too busy to schedule a timely meeting. To her credit, Dame Billie met with me almost immediately. She made it perfectly clear she accepted the Aristide version of events and she remained intractable on the issue, even when I suggested her position was tantamount to calling the U.S. secretary of state a liar. This was hard for me to understand and even harder to accept.

In spite of our differences, later in the day I was invited to attend the COFCOR meeting which was scheduled to be held in Barbados with Dame Billie presiding. I listened to speech after speech regarding the situation in Haiti. All blaming the U.S. for kidnapping Aristide and the ensuing collapse of the Haitian society. They conveniently forgot the collapse of the society was the cause of Aristide fleeing the country for his own safety. They also neglected to mention that none of them offered him asylum, believing he would be a disruptive force in the region. *What a mess.* After the gathering, several of my fellow diplomats mentioned how carefully the speakers phrased their words out of deference to my attendance. *Really.* I'd hate to hear what would have been said if I had not been there!

The evening event for this group was a lavish and elaborate cocktail reception and dinner on the beach at the Savannah Hotel. Dame Billie, ever the gracious hostess, seated me at her table along with the Speaker of the U.N. General Assembly, at that time Julian Hunte from St. Lucia. The table conversation was very interesting regarding the taint of corruption at the U.N., including the administration of the General Assembly. Hunte said he intended to institute some efficiencies and reforms. Everyone wished him success because everyone knew corruption knew no bounds and inefficiencies were rampant. Improvements were desperately needed.

When the Caribbean leaders immediately and with unanimity accepted the Aristide version of events, it was shocking to me, to DOS staff in Washington and to many of my colleagues in the diplomatic corps as well. There was an immediate and unanimous acceptance of one side of the story, along with intractable refusal to listen to the other side. Was I naïve to be shocked? Perhaps. But I didn't stay naive for long. My cynicism increased and my respect diminished exponentially.

These small countries believe there is no behavior egregious enough to bring about regime change through international intervention. They believe there is nothing that justifies international intervention anywhere in the world—not horrific, continuing human rights violations, not ethnic cleansing, not failed leadership, not bloody coups, not corruption, not genocide. Whether or not leaders are elected or have put themselves in place by force; no matter if they are despots or international outlaws, they must not be challenged. The insurgency in Haiti had already brought about regime change. Continuing to defend and support a failed government was not possible. The critical question that followed was who could govern Haiti in the aftermath.

Perhaps being leaders of small fragile nations made them feel that way. Clearly they felt this was an issue that went against their best interest and they reacted in a way they felt served their best interests. As a matter of fact, the U.S. government rarely takes an action that is not in our best interests either.

Even after their stinging public tongue lashings, they expected no consequences, no change in the bilateral relationship with the U.S. Indeed, requests for assistance of all kinds continued unabated and it was clearly the expectation that U.S. largesse would continue; that search and rescue efforts would continue to be performed on demand, free flow of goods and people from their countries to the U.S. would be uninterrupted and the U.S. would continue to serve as the preferred first emergency responder. All these things would continue, with no strings or expectations after all the vitriolic rhetoric. For me, a Midwesterner with a certain sense of fairness and reciprocity, this was a difficult pill to swallow. They all continued to trumpet the message to me. "We are your friends, we share your values." By that time I thought, *"Sure you do."*

This was a difficult but important lesson that served me well and illuminated my thinking regarding the degree of friendship or trust that could be expected from CARICOM leaders. They were not reliable allies; they could not be counted on to take a stand on issues, to respond positively to requests for support for U.S. positions or to reciprocate our assistance in any way. In the words of one, "We're small nations, we can't be expected to support, _____." *You fill in the blank.*

A similar issue was the position these nations took regarding Cuba. Their own respect for human rights and their passion for their independence were completely contradictory in their treatment of Castro and Cuba. When asked to vote on a United Nations resolution condemning human rights violations in Cuba, the Prime Minister of St. Lucia opined "I can't vote against Fidel, he sends me doctors."

Thankfully, it was still early in my posting. I had a new understanding and appreciation of the wisdom of former President Reagan. "Trust, but verify." All in my endlessly pleasant mode, of course.

It was a remarkable experience to live out of the country and come to understand how grass roots citizens view the U.S. In the Caribbean, the U.S. is largely considered that territory that includes Miami, Washington, D.C., and New York. Some people also know of the Carolinas because they have had work permits there to learn the "tourist industry." Still, the appetite for visas or all kinds and the expectation that the U.S. government would always do the "right" thing, according to their definition of the "right" thing, demonstrated the persons on the street respected the U.S., enjoyed knowing our citizens who came as tourists and dreamed of sharing that "good life."

CHAPTER EIGHT

TACKLING A BROKEN SYSTEM, ONE INCH OF RED TAPE AT A TIME

It was very clear there was a very direct and very public connection between embassy actions and the resulting perceptions of our competence and the cause of diplomacy, our ability to get things done. Even the behind-the-scenes, seemingly inconsequential things like administrative processes directly affected our ability to do our jobs and had an impact upon the image we promoted. We often appeared to be inefficient, and in some cases incompetent, largely due to lack of attention to process management. Smart, articulate, highly motivated people were nearly paralyzed by the tools they were given, and America looked bad in the process. My bias for action just didn't allow for standing by while a badly broken system continued to flourish. So I considered: What could one Irish grandmother do to make a difference at a small embassy in the Caribbean?

The insularity that exists between departments and agencies, and the lack of meaningful communication between DOS and embassies creates huge problems that lead to frustration, inefficiency and waste. Bureaucrats in Washington make unilateral decisions, never consulting with the field, and with little or no idea or even interest in how those decisions will play out. Whether it was budget reductions or the archaic demands of outdated administrative processes, there was seemingly no interest in continuous improvement or in learning how decisions might actually affect those out in the field. It was the epitome of classic "top-down unconscious incompetence." Meaning "they don't know (unconscious) what they don't know (incompetence)." Since I had no career aspirations, I saw little personal risk and decided to become a very "squeaky wheel." I could at least make sure there was *awareness* of the consequences of those top-down decisions. That might rise to the level of *"conscious* incompetence," meaning they *know* what they don't know. I didn't know how to make people care. It was very difficult to accept the lack of individual accountability for decisions. In fact, it was usually impossible to learn *when* or *why* a decision was made or even who made it. Announcements just came down from "on high" (usually in a cable), sometimes several months after the fact.

Many of the processes, procedures, and systems used by the DOS and the embassy were antiquated and inefficient, unrelated to any "best practices" experienced over my years in the business community. Make no mistake; my life experience had given me a clear understanding of the differences between government and business. Attempting to run government "like a business" is not a good answer. In business, when something becomes unprofitable or no longer of interest to the customer, one can stop doing it. In government many services must be provided, so the task is to manage them as efficiently and effectively as possible. But there is no reason for government to eschew good management practices and remain stuck in the past. These policies and issues did not come from *years* of bureaucratic paralysis; they came from *decades* of bureaucratic paralysis. I do not single out the DOS in these criticisms. I found the same to be true wherever I went in Washington and with nearly all the agencies represented at the embassy. When I expressed my frustration to my colleagues, I was often told "It is frustrating, but State is better than most." I did not take comfort from that. My bias for action, which created controversy from time to time, took over and I sought areas where I could be an effective change agent. Embassy Bridgetown was a small post. We did not attract much interest or attention from Washington, so after I had studied the systems and processes we had to work with, I began to question what we could do for ourselves that would make us more productive and effective and make our work more efficient and satisfying personally.

Communication dysfunction affected nearly every administrative process used by the embassy. As I quickly learned, everything we did, from the dramatic work of assisting Grenada to recover from Hurricane Ivan, to very small gestures recognizing our own employees, could either forward the cause of diplomacy or send it backward months, if not years.

Take the issue of employee reassignment and promotion. Americans assigned overseas go to a new post every three years or so. Turnover, that is people leaving government service, was much higher than it should have been because of the lack of value some decision-makers in Washington placed on employees and their needs. Length of service was determined on the "hardship" conditions at the post. For instance, Baghdad, one year, Bogota, two years, Barbados, three years, London four years. And how perverse is a process that means the most complex and difficult locations have the highest "planned" turnover? Never mind the turnover that occurs as people leave the service. A family may be given just three days to decide where they will move for the next three-year posting. No provision was made for allowing children to complete the school year or for an employed spouse to give notice. If they felt they simply could not accept the new posting, families would correctly conclude they had no recourse but to leave the Foreign Service. This was a tragic failure, one that damaged the cause of diplomacy and democracy. People with great potential and bright futures, who had been provided extensive (and expensive) training in language and diplomatic relations, were lost in this unfortunate process. Getting a return on investment from that very high quality education and training provided at the Foreign Service Institute was not considered a high priority.

The same issue created endless headaches on the other side of the desk. From a management perspective, losing a third of the embassy staff every year presented a significant challenge—think of the time and cost involved in retraining new employees. But imagine if one of those people had to cut short their time or service for other reasons; a family emergency or a personal health problem. We might get a temporary substitute, but there would be no replacement until the next "cycle." Obviously, there was no chance for DOS to get a return on its training investments. Even in the "planned" turnover, a staff member would leave for a fresh assignment and his or her replacement wouldn't arrive for months, leaving the other team members to carry on the additional work, or having to leave work undone. This was an antiquated and harmful system all around.

Cross training was a partial solution to the turnover problem. Employees understood the more skills and training they had, the more valuable they became, and so they welcomed additional information. If they carried an absent colleague's load for two to three months until a replacement arrived, they could help train the newcomer and made themselves more valuable. This was not a systemic solution or even a good solution to the problem, but it was a fairly simple method of getting our work done and provided a method of serving the best interest of our employees.

The problem for families was intractable and more poignant, and I had no way of making change. My only recourse was to voice my displeasure over the method of placing people in overseas assignments in a way that left only a very narrow window for families to choose where they had to settle on a new home. And I was careful how I did that because I could potentially damage the employee relationship with the "bureaucracy" if someone thought the employee was encouraging me to advocate on their behalf. And wasn't that perverse? I was warned that my advocating for outstanding employees could label that employee in a negative way. *Ouch!*

About this time I experienced some serious turnover of my own. It was time for Marcia to return to Washington for her next assignment. Thankfully, I was able to help select her replacement. Like Marcia, Meg Gilroy was a senior Foreign Service professional, and she became a great new teammate and friend. Having just come from assignment in Washington, she knew who and where to call for information. And Meg's husband Harlie and Kay became great friends as well. They nominated themselves S.I.R., meaning Spouses In Residence. They even had business cards printed!

The next big loss was Bonita. According to DOS, it was time for Bonita to retire. I had delayed that event for a year by insisting she was needed since I was so new to the job, but that excuse ran out. So, I sadly and gratefully had to say farewell to Bonita.

I had great respect for the woman who was the OMS in the Political/ Economic office down the hall and decided to ask her to move into my office. She graciously accepted and proved herself worthy of that promotion every single day thereafter. But, apparently promoting from within the embassy was just not done. I fear I caused Nancy some hardship with the "higher-ups" in the DOS later on. What were they thinking? She should have declined? Nancy's husband Peter worked as a consultant at the NEC. He was a Scottish gentleman with a wonderful accent and a tremendous knowledge and experience with large construction projects.

So in spite of two huge losses we had two wonderful new teammates and friends. It's hard to express how thankful I am for Marcia and Bonita and Meg and Nancy. They all contributed in a big way to my productivity and my goal achievement. I'm proud to say they have become lasting friends (BFFs) as well.

Many international businesses manage this necessary transfer process successfully. Surely it would not be too difficult for someone to research "best practices" and make recommendations for change. But again, no one felt any responsibility to even study this issue. The culture of continuous improvement simply did not exist.

I *could* address the pressing need for an American school in Bridgetown. Recruitment of families with young (up to primary school age) children was possible. Families with older children were wary of a system that tracked children into middle and secondary schools using their scores on the "Eleven

Plus Exam." I first turned to the International School folks for assistance and they were very helpful, but it became apparent after several months of study that a standalone school at a small Post like Barbados likely would not be self-sustaining. So what were the alternatives? Happily we were able to collaborate with Codrington School, a local school with a great reputation, founded in the early 1700s. Through some of the American families who had chosen to send their children to Codrington, I learned there was interest in introducing the international baccalaureate curriculum, a curriculum used in prestigious schools world-wide. The School Committee of the embassy joined forces with the Codrington Board of Directors and by the time I left, Codrington had introduced the international curriculum for several grade levels in the school and planned to add a grade each year. It was a great local partnership that offered a very attractive alternative for American families coming to Barbados. In past attempts, the Barbados Ministry of Education had opposed starting an American School, assuming it would become a haven for rich white families, even though at least half the families who came to Barbados to work at the embassy were people of color. Our partnership with Codrington had the added benefit of demonstrating our commitment to quality education for all children.

Annually we were expected to follow a convoluted process called the MPP, Mission Performance Plan. Initially I thought this sounded like a useful exercise. Then I learned the required software package used to complete this task was so convoluted and dysfunctional, it required us to assign an economic officer nearly full time for several months. Since there were only three political/economic officers in Bridgetown to cover our seven countries, we really couldn't afford to have one of them stop doing their daily work to focus on this, but there was little alternative. Next great revelation: We were expected to complete this work with no idea of either the financial or human resource we could expect to have available. The assignment: *Create a vision of the desired future for Embassy Bridgetown without knowing what funds or people would be available to accomplish it.* Kind of like bowling with a curtain in front of the pins. Some years back someone gave me a glittery magic wand decorated with bright pink feathers that flashed and jingled when turned on...even that could not fix this process.

We dutifully completed the project, not doing so would have been extremely career damaging for any DOS employee at Post. We filled in all the appropriate blanks using our current budget and human resource allotments as a baseline. We also attempted to demonstrate how making some process changes would improve our efficiency and effectiveness and allow us to add some additional programs without adding people or cost. We thought if we increased productivity, we could do more with the same resources. We tried to choose projects that would suit each of our countries current situations, as described in the strategic plan we had developed for each nation. Our suggestions also reflected a philosophy of helping people to help themselves. All the agencies got involved in the process so we could better understand what the military, USAID and others brought to the table in terms of ideas and resources. Then we submitted our MPP. Only once in the three years did we receive any feedback. Each year I insisted the number one priority of the embassy was focused on the president's directive to me—maintain stable democracies. The only feedback we ever received occurred when someone at DOS disagreed with that as our number one priority. No individual called to discuss it. Instead, a video conference was scheduled. We were to have all our country team members at the table—that was a lot of people. As it turned out, there were even more DOS people at the table in Washington than we had in Bridgetown. *Big meeting.* The person who called the meeting introduced himself and began talking. No one else was introduced, either by name or by responsibility. I interrupted to suggest it would be helpful if we knew who we were speaking to and requested both groups go around the table, introduce themselves and state their area of responsibility. That was done. At least we knew the players. But it soon became apparent that discussion of our number one priority goal was the only agenda item for the meeting. When the priority issue was questioned, I insisted on maintaining our position. I expressed my opinion that the goal had been given to me, the COM, by the president and that made it number one. No one else spoke, even when I requested feedback from the people in both rooms. End of discussion. I think I began to earn my reputation here. *"Mary, Mary, Quite Contrary."*

The DOS program budget for Embassy Bridgetown, to be used in all seven countries, was reduced by at least one third each of the three years I served. We learned what our budget would be by cable, usually about six months into the fiscal year. There was no opportunity for adjustment or discussion. Along with the numbers came a very clear command in all capital letters and bold print. *"SHOW NO RETRENCHMENT."* I was reminded of dancing partners Fred Astaire and Ginger Rogers. Fred got most of the credit, but Ginger did everything he did, backwards and in high heels. *To my way of thinking DOS was Fred and the embassies were Ginger!*

The amount of budget we needed to be even marginally effective was pitifully small. In many cases, support for small projects, say the purchase and presentation of cake decorating tools for a culinary class, training workers for positions in the tourist industry could make a huge impact in both relationship with the government and at the grass roots level. It added and preserved jobs. We scraped together some funds and made a presentation. Great feedback and wonderful media coverage. We also got great feedback from the learners.

There was a cottage industry made up of women who stitched bedding and draperies for hotels and bed and breakfasts. Sewing machines for these entrepreneurs could enlarge the number of people at work exponentially, and there was a great demand for their products. Could not get it done.

As you have gathered by now, I did not go quietly when I advocated for these projects. I called, emailed, even made advocacy trips to Washington from time to time. I learned to my dismay that accountability for funding such programs was so obtuse, it was very difficult to find anyone who would admit that funds for an idea or a project came under their purview. "Not *my* job," "No funds in *my* budget," "Not *my* idea," "Let me get back to you on that," were the responses I received. Paralysis by analysis!

Thanks to the tenacity of our public affairs officer, we received a grant from her department to purchase a collection of books, which we presented to the public libraries on several of our islands in celebration of Martin Luther King's birthday. She worked with each library to set up a reading corner featuring these books. I was invited to come and read to children during the children's hour on Saturday mornings. My visits received full and positive coverage from all the local media. Because this resonated so strongly, I was asked to visit schools to read as well. This was such a small thing, but was so well received that during my farewell to Post, I was presented with beautifully framed and autographed pictures of me reading to children. *I loved doing it.*

The Regional Security System (RSS) was a collaboration of all seven countries' military forces that was designed to be called in when a country faced a big problem, natural disaster, jail fire, ship sinking, anything that would overpower a single country's resources. It was one of the few collaborative initiatives that really worked. The headquarters was located in Barbados, and the Barbados government provided offices, training facilities, and warehouse space. Our military liaison officer arranged for a team of law enforcement officers from the RSS to receive training in deep water search and rescue efforts. Relevant and useful training. At the end of the training, the equipment used during the classes was donated to the team. I went to the "graduation" ceremonies to present the equipment to the group. Both the commissioner of police and the attorney general attended to express their thanks. Once again, outstanding media coverage.

My point? Thoughtful, small contributions of direct assistance, along with relevant training experiences, had the potential to make a very big difference. They added jobs, and they improved relationships with our governments, and since they impacted grass roots citizens, they helped in winning hearts and minds. And when contributions came with technical training and preparation so that the learners were capable of carrying on independently with the tools provided, we were able to create positive change not only for one day but for the future. Relevance made people at the grass roots believe we were listening, we cared, we were engaged and understood their needs. It became more difficult for elected officials to point fingers or blame the U.S. for all their ills and problems. *When we are credible, negative rhetoric is not.*

Budget decisions had no relationship to any plan or strategy we submitted. Funding for valuable programs could disappear without warning at any time of the budget cycle. Sometimes line items that included salary funds for employees disappeared too. This meant that individual employees and their families had to move when the funding for their position was cut. When that happened, they did not have the opportunity to be a part of the usual "transfer" process and had to take whatever openings were available—anywhere in the world. Once again, the U.S. government was often the loser, as gifted employees left government service to find employment elsewhere.

Members of Congress often micromanage the allocation of funds. No surprise there, it's a fact of life. If one "followed the money," one learned there was usually a "fact finding" trip to that location in the works. So the member of Congress would complete the allocation and several months later would arrive in country, sometimes with an entourage, receive the red carpet treatment from various local government officials, be thanked effusively for their "gifts" to the people of the country and then stay and enjoy the royal treatment for a few days of beach and sunshine. Meantime, embassy staff members scurry to make appropriate hotel and meal arrangements, create the appointment schedule with the government officials and respond to questions as to why the embassy was not better prepared. These no-win situations were a real test of my "endlessly pleasant" personality.

Politics were everywhere, and Washington had the champions. From my own political experience I could see that certain DOS employees had built personal relationships with members of Congress or their staffs that provided them an inside track to influence budget allocations. So sometimes a person near the top of a "silo" had an inordinate, yet anonymous, influence on the allocation of funds. It was prudent of them to be sure the "touch of their hand" was never visible.

Passing a Federal budget, or avoiding passing a budget, added another degree of difficulty to the dysfunction of the embassy. Each year I was at Post, Congress failed to pass a budget in a timely fashion, and so we operated under a continuing resolution. Continuing resolutions cause near paralysis in the field. Here's the way it works. With a continuing resolution, embassies are told they should operate as if they had the same funds they received the previous year. This would be fine, except the experienced people knew there were huge pitfalls. When a budget was actually passed, if funds for an embassy or a program were cut or eliminated, other money had to be found within the embassy budget, in the few months of the fiscal year that were left, to avoid overspending. And if the allocation was the *same* amount or through some miracle, *more* than the previous year, there would be a rush to spend it, because all unexpended funds had to be returned to D.C. so that DOS folks could distribute it where they thought it was most needed. A classic definition: "Damned if you do, and damned if you don't." While I was willing to risk taking local initiative to reallocate money to programs and activities we knew were effective, I understood that would create a huge career "risk" for the career people around me. There would be those in Washington who would expect my colleagues to *prevent* me from making funding decisions and the consequences for my staff could be dire. Sometimes the consequences would be as serious as creating a "tick" in the personnel folder that would ensure they would be cycled out of the DOS at the first opportunity. But that's for another chapter. I told staff, "If there are career risks to be taken, let me take them. I have NO career aspirations, so feel free to say the devil (or the ambassador) made me do it."

In the world of business, the cable is called a memorandum. But in Washington, cables had a very rigid, very specific format. The ability to "write a cable," completing all the coding, i.e., the jargon on the first few pages, was actually a line item on the performance evaluation form. Neither the jargon nor the evaluation topic measured substance, it involved following the approved format. It reminded me that *some people insist that children must always be taught to color within the lines.*

When I arrived, our political and economic officers humorously referred to themselves as a "fax factory." Because of the volume of incoming cables from Washington asking embassy staff members to get response from their host government, the only real option was for the Political/Economic department of the embassy to identify which ones needed to be shared with which governments. They often had to send these requests on to all seven governments. The foreign ministries of our small nations usually had only one or two diplomats on staff. Yet, we were expected to ascertain their official positions on Rwanda, Myanmar, Antarctica, or whatever the many issues of the day were, and report back to Washington. We simply flooded these countries with requests for information. We would fax requests for information off to whatever named person we had on record. That person might or might not still have been employed. Often there was no response, so no one really ever knew if they were received or read. If Washington expected some action from the local government, phone calls were made in an attempt to follow up. It was the only way they knew how to deal with the volume of paperwork that came across their desks day after day. Obviously, this was not a very effective way to get information, to make requests or to gain support for whatever issue we were dealing with at the time.

The cable was another classic example of "we've always done it that way." The format had no doubt been effective and efficient when communications had to be telegraphed. Today, all cables are transmitted through email channels, yet no one has seen the need or felt empowered to suggest changes. Cables came in two flavors, open and classified. As things stood, political and economic officers and other agency heads reviewed *all* the cables arriving on the open system. DCM Marcia then received nearly all of them and spent a good deal of her time determining what should be done with them. If they required action, someone had to be assigned not only to take the action but to write a report or make a call regarding what they learned. All classified cables, except those directed to a specific agency, were handled through the "front" office. That front office consisted of the ambassador and her OMS, and the DCM and her OMS.

Agency heads within the embassy often received similar classified cables on the same subject from their chain of command. Their messages were not always consistent with the messages from DOS to the front office, so clarification of the substance of the message and the process of our response required meeting time.

Nearly every cable that arrived was labeled as High Priority, and demanded immediate action, or urgent reporting back to D.C. *Everything* was urgent and high priority. Because we were the only embassy in the world with responsibility for seven countries, it was impossible for the available staff to respond to these directives in a timely manner. Providing information to all seven of our countries in a timely manner was almost impossible under these circumstances.

This created yet another career risk for our people. Because Bridgetown was a very small post, often the most "junior" officers were assigned there. This would usually be their second or third posting, after they had completed the obligatory first posting in consular affairs. Some people in Washington judged that failure to respond immediately to these demands resulted in an unsatisfactory performance. As we analyzed the depth and the breadth, the sheer quantity of the cable traffic, every process improvement we considered had to be weighed against our capacity to respond.

It was apparent that there were individuals and groups within DOS who justified their existence by sending cables and making demands. Some cables were intended only to provide background information; so-called "briefings" on issues or current events around the world (they were never brief). These needed to be routed and read by the appropriate people. Some were messages that were intended to be delivered by the embassy to one or all of our governments. Others demanded that someone in the embassy, a foreign service officer, the DCM or the ambassador personally deliver the message by phone or by a face to face meeting.

Throughout the embassy, over 200 cables (usually from 10 to 20 pages apiece) arrived every week so the *process* of how to manage all this information and take any requested action became almost as important as the substance of the issues, at least for the near term.

We needed to create a streamlined, effective process, and we did. If you're easily bored with process improvement talk, skip over the next few paragraphs. I describe them here only because I was delighted with the changes and found it amazing how much more efficient and effective we could be with only small process changes.

For the open system cables, the political economic staff was assigned the first sort, they determined what was for information only and notified whoever needed to see it. Electronic files were developed that stored those cables for one week so they could be read or retrieved by people who needed to see them. Those cables that requested or demanded action were delivered to the DCM twice a day. She reviewed them, determined which ones should be handled by others in the embassy, and which ones she or I needed to deal with personally. At the end of that meeting the officers returned to their desks to handle the assignments that came their way. Every morning, all the classified cables, were reviewed by the OMS in the front office. They prioritized them, talked to agency heads if clarification was needed and gave them to me and the DCM.

The "cable" meeting usually determined my schedule for the rest of the day, and often most of the next morning. Making calls, scheduling meetings, making travel arrangements for face-to-face meetings, etc. Through the wonders of technology and the fact that I never traveled without a staff member, we could maintain this process whether we were in the office or not. When traveling, the classified information was usually delivered to me by the DCM.

We became much more efficient and effective. The copy and fax machines got a rest; our cost for paper went down. Faxes stopped rolling out to our countries and important issues got the attention and follow up they deserved. After a few weeks using this process, staff was comfortable making quick, thoughtful judgments about who to call and what to recommend.

By the time DCM Marcia left and DCM Meg Gilroy arrived, the process was habit. The team effect had taken over and Meg took over leadership without missing a beat. It took a bit of extra time when new team members arrived because the way we were doing business was a bit unusual. We also worked to create a culture where it was clear someone more senior was always available and actually encouraged people to seek consultation or advice. This kind of focused and disciplined process management served us well.

It became clear almost immediately to government officials in our countries that something was different. The faxes were far fewer and were for information only. Action items were handled by telephone. Meetings were requested when appropriate. The change was obvious and positive.

This did not prevent some of the officials in our countries from continuing their practice of trying to dodge calls or avoid scheduling meetings. A few still made themselves scarce; especially in matters when media coverage had provided clues about what the issue would likely be. If they wanted to avoid taking a position, or they didn't want to be held accountable for their public remarks or for the problems they had created, their schedules were full. I learned that when Bonita or Nancy called on my behalf, assistants were more likely to say the boss was busy or gone for the day. However, if I placed the call myself, the assistant often became so flustered, I was immediately transferred to the official I was calling, sometimes much to his distress. Of course, when they came to the phone, they were always "delighted" to hear from me. *Sure they were.*

I found some of the human resource policies at DOS so difficult and unfair, I feel compelled to write about them. Fair warning, you may not find it interesting or important. Just speed read the next few pages.

Three areas in particular had my attention.

I was told to cut the pay of DOS staff across the board, with no notice. An assistant secretary for administration paid us a visit. We had prepared and presented all the information she had requested, and provided gracious hospitality. During our exit briefing, she told us how much she admired the changes we had made and complimented us on the very high morale at Post. She could see this was a very effective embassy. *Wow, that felt really good.* High praise indeed. I accompanied her to the airport. While she was being escorted to her plane to return to Washington, she sent one of her staff people to catch me before I left the airport. The young man tapped on my car window as Peter was driving me away from the airport. Of course, the windows do not go down in the armored car, so we stopped and I got out. "The Secretary neglected to tell you that pay for DOS employees will be cut by five percent, effective immediately. It will show in their next paycheck, so you will need to inform by next Tuesday." WHAT? Too late for a face to face meeting about this, she was already on the plane. I tried to overturn this decision, or at least delay it for several months until the current group left Post and new arrivals could be prepared. Pay promises are sacred. When an individual or a young family came to Barbados, which is an outrageously expensive place to live, they were told what salary they could expect for the year. Then I was directed to inform them "no matter how well you are performing, your pay will be cut immediately because the money is needed elsewhere." By any standards, this lacked integrity and broke a promise. It also sent a clear, dreadful message about how the human resource is valued—or not. *I have often been frustrated with my government, but this was the first time I was ashamed of it.*

Another example involved the performance appraisal systems. The person being evaluated first wrote a review of their performance. This was read by their immediate superior, and that individual wrote an evaluation of that performance. The paperwork then went to the DCM, who read the appraisal and added comments. Finally it came to me. I read all the previous work and made appropriate comments. OK, it was not necessary or expected for me to write anything, but I felt I owed it to these bright, hardworking young people to add my view of a positive performance. Not through yet. An appointed review committee at Post then reviewed all the performance appraisals (what happened to confidentiality?) and suggested "edits." For instance, if there was no sentence about working well with superiors, the review boards in Washington would assume the person did NOT work well with superiors. After all this wordsmithing, the appraisal was sent to Washington, where it was reviewed by *yet another committee* of peers. Only then (in Washington) were salary recommendations added. Salary recommendations were made by persons three levels away from actual management. This process took many man hours over many *months*. Any comments on the appraisal form that suggested ways to improve a performance were a death knell for the person being reviewed. It was always appropriate to say something like "This person just works too hard," as if it were a criticism. I learned that actual coaching should be done verbally face-to-face and one-on-one. I made my written comments fit expectations perfectly. This type of review process caused much consternation all the while it was going on because it was obvious nearly everyone at Post would be privy to what was written. Rarely do I find things that are perfect, but this system was the *perfect* recipe for "happy talk" appraisals. *If the purpose of performance appraisal is to improve performance, (and why else should it exist?), this system fails on every count.*

Time to get off my soapbox about processes and employee policies. To many people, performance appraisal systems, transfer policies, salary policies and the deluge of cables that were received daily may seem of little consequence, boring even. But these were urgent and emotional issues that directly impacted the performance of our personnel and their families abroad. People are the front line for diplomacy abroad, and they joined the Foreign Service to serve their country. We worked with people who had great potential and were well motivated. They received excellent, extensive, and expensive training in language and diplomatic relations. Many of them chose to leave the Foreign Service after their first three to five years, largely due to these unfortunate processes. I am often asked to write a recommendation for folks as they prepare to leave the DOS. I feel a sense of loss and wonder why it became necessary. As I said before, many international companies have exemplary human resource policies. A "best practices" review of those policies and adoption of some common sense changes would make a world of difference.

Bottom line overall? These antiquated processes are merely the by-products of a system that needs complete overhaul from the top down. *Why doesn't somebody do something?* Because a bureaucracy just keeps on doing what it's programmed to do until something or someone intervenes.

Most of the top people at federal agencies serve at the pleasure of the president and consider themselves policy people. Unless they are not being properly served, they stay focused on policy and have nothing to do with management. If they receive data and information where and when they need it, they see no need to change anything. Certainly they do not see it as their responsibility. Of the 8,000 positions appointed by a president, few have any interest in instituting the kind of process improvements that create a more efficient and effective system. Meanwhile, many career people simply adopted a "this too shall pass" mentality. There is no incentive at all for seeking change; in fact, to do so would be "career threatening." They know that if they just hang in there, another appointee will soon arrive and that person needs to rely on them to learn the ropes. It's a never-ending cycle. Without interested and demanding leadership, no one is prepared to take any initiative to make things better.

Little wonder. The incentive for bureaucrats, no matter how well motivated, is to maintain the status quo and serve up whatever is requested in a timely way: longevity and tenure, not productivity or innovation, are the measures of accomplishment and achievement. Process improvements are never considered, except when budget decisions require cuts. Even then the usual response is cut "across the board" because that method does not require prioritizing or explanation. Meaningful change is rarely accomplished, and the human resource policies, among others, are locked somewhere in the 1950s. It often appears those who are not well motivated or productive flourish in such an environment.

So much positive change could occur if government leaders would lead. There is only one chance for real change to occur. It would require an administration that accepted the need to institute a continuous improvement culture, who would appoint some people with *management* goals and objectives. Persons who would see it as their responsibility to identify areas of improvement and institute changes. At Embassy Bridgetown when we did that, even in our small place, we got results that extended well beyond the Caribbean. I saw firsthand how management changes transformed individuals, teams, efficiency and execution, and how they forwarded diplomatic efforts. They increased satisfaction for staff members. There is much at stake. We stand to lose more than we can fathom if our government processes aren't overhauled so that embassies are able to operate efficiently, skillfully, and respectfully.

CHAPTER NINE

THE POWER OF DIPLOMACY

One of my most effective diplomatic tools was to address people directly. From the outset I intended to be an ambassador who was actively involved, who wasn't shielded by layers of handlers or who made only occasional, carefully scripted public appearances. I knew the buck stopped with me, and I felt a responsibility to deal with problems directly and immediately. This hands-on style, coupled with my Iowa down to earth approach, helped me when several thorny issues presented themselves.

Late in my first year, everyone at the embassy, me at the top of the list, was blind sided with a public relations disaster. A front page article in the Barbados Nation newspaper reported that a travel advisory had appeared on the State Department website that recommended Americans not travel to Barbados, and lambasted the Barbados police, calling them "incompetent, nonresponsive, and uncaring." Those were fighting words, and untrue. The State Department website gathered information submitted from embassies all over the world and publicized situations where Americans should be aware of escalated travel risk. Our annual travel information relating to Barbados and our other countries had been submitted to Washington as required and we had received no notification of anything being amiss. *Someone in DOS had added these untrue words without telling us!* Public officials and private citizens were livid, and the embassy was inundated with complaints. I called a meeting of the country team and made a shocking pronouncement: "There is a huge crow in the middle of this table and we are going to eat every bite of it!" Several members of the team tried to dissuade me from admitting this was a mistake or even attempting to fix it, arguing that doing so would portray weakness.

I disagreed and asked Consul General Bob Fretz to do two things. First, call a news conference for that afternoon and announce that the traveler information sheet was in error and had been published without our knowledge. *We had not made those comments.* And second, since the travelers information function was in his "silo," I asked him to get it corrected by the end of business that day. I personally called Attorney General Mottley (who had oversight of police matters) and asked her to refrain from public comment until we could get this mistake fixed. She agreed. Marcia and RSO Dan Becker personally delivered a letter of apology to the commissioner of police that afternoon. We turned a big challenge into an opportunity. No one thought the "arrogant Americans" would ever admit a mistake and fix it, nor did they think we would ever publicly apologize. When we did, our apologies were graciously accepted. The media, who had been attending regular luncheons at the residence, covered the story in a balanced way. There were those in Washington who were not pleased with our handling of this incident. I was told it might have been better to just let the storm blow over. *Wrong!* We won friends and took another big step in rehabilitating our image abroad. It was a lesson in diplomacy that I learned at my father's knee: when you're wrong, admit it, say you are sorry and fix it. Immediately. Then make sure it does not happen again. That last thing proved the most difficult. No one would admit to putting the information on the website. We never learned who created the problem.

Agents with the Drug Enforcement Agency (DEA) briefed me regarding two men who had been identified as drug kingpins in the U.S. and who had been avoiding their fate by hiding out in the Caribbean. This had been a problem for over ten years. By the time the problem arrived on my desk, the drug lords had appealed to the Privy Council in London for the third and final time and were awaiting ruling. Meanwhile, during my credential presentation, it became clear that the St. Kitts government was not especially motivated to help us return these guys to the U.S. I made a visit to St. Kitts and chose my words carefully. I expressed my concern to the St. Kitts Prime Minister and his attorney general, and explained that it would be very difficult for the U.S. government to continue to do business with a government that harbored dangerous criminals. This got their attention, as I expected. They understood the Grandma from Iowa was not going to let this one slide. I asked politely again "How many appeals did you say were still available to them?" The answer, "One." I continued "And in your opinion, what is the chance of them being acquitted?" "None," came the answer. So I said, "Then we will watch with interest as the court makes its final ruling and we will watch with interest how your government handles this verdict as well. We stand ready to provide assistance to return these men to the U.S. at any time."

A few months later, it became publicly known that the final appeal was lost. The prime minister called and told me the court case was over but that he was unwilling to move the men because of his concern over DEA's methods. They would be "too disruptive." When I pressed for specifics about his concerns with DEA agents, he could not come up with any, so I suspected he was still trying to avoid taking any action. I sensed we had made marginal progress, but I also realized it might be possible to solve a long-standing problem without damaging a fragile but improving relationship with his government. So, rather than defend the DEA, deny his statement or accuse him of evasion, I asked, "How would you *prefer* for these men to be removed? I am prepared to offer my personal assistance to make this go smoothly." Momentary silence.

Then suddenly, he proposed a solution. He would select members of his law enforcement detail to make the arrests and escort the men to the airport, where DEA agents would be waiting with a U.S. plane. He wanted the handover and the takeoff to occur after dark. After consulting with the DEA Director James Doby, I agreed and left the ball in his court. We would wait to hear from him. He called the very next day and requested a plane for that evening. The situation played out exactly as he requested, and a ten-year-old problem for St. Kitts and the U.S. vanished without a ripple.

Article 98 of the Rome Statutes of the International Court is an article that describes how military personnel who are arrested outside their home country are to be handled. The article states they will first be tried in the country where they are arrested for whatever civil crime they are accused of. They are subject to the laws and the punishment meted out in that country. If law enforcement is not functioning due to war or civil unrest, or when a verdict is appealed, the case will be turned over to the International Court. Most Caribbean countries relied on the British Privy Council as their Supreme Court, but they also accepted the jurisdiction of the International Court at The Hague. We were asking them to sign a U.S. document that basically said if there was no functioning legal system in a country, due to war or anarchy, or if there was a conviction and an appeal followed, the accused individual must be placed under U.S. jurisdiction, and be returned to the U.S. for trial, thus eliminating any role for the International Court. This is a constitutional issue for the U.S., but many countries considered it an attempt to protect members of the U.S. military from accountability for their behavior when serving abroad. It was well known at home and abroad that members of our military rarely misbehave themselves while serving overseas, but the Pentagon did not want to place our men and women in potential legal jeopardy.

To make it even more problematic, Congress had passed a law prohibiting the distribution of funds from certain programs that provided U.S. military aid or training to countries that refused to sign. After arriving at Post and completing credential presentations, the calls from Washington began, pressuring me to make Article 98 signatures the priority issue that drove all others. The callers also demanded aid be stopped immediately for those nations that refused. It was the only issue where Washington staff applied constant pressure with calls and communications asking for progress reports. "What have you done for me today?" kinds of questions. There were regular calls at the office and sometimes evening or weekend calls at the residence. If my efforts were deemed unsatisfactory, I was rather forcefully requested to visit prime ministers with this item as the sole topic. Staff from this group would expect to accompany me on these visits. Immediate reporting of results was expected. Of interest to me, the Article 98 issue was scarcely mentioned during my training process. Yet it became one of the most divisive and difficult issues confronting me at Post. Island government officials felt this was at best heavy handed and at worst, blackmail. And, they believed it was being pursued because the U.S. did not want members of their military to be subject to the same behavior standards as the rest of the world. This was an incorrect interpretation of the document, but it was the perception I faced. To make matters worse, after listening to some of my fellow ambassadors and some military leaders, I began to question whether the DOS, the military and the administration were on the same page on this issue.

For some desperate countries there was no gasoline for law enforcement vehicles and boats even in the rare moments when they were in operating condition. Law enforcement personnel had no ammunition for their weapons. In Dominica, a party of fisher-folk drowned because the government was unable to perform search and rescue missions. Desperate people do desperate things. Those desperate things are not always in the best interest of the U.S. Turning to Venezuela and the People's Republic of China for assistance was one alternative, but with them, there was a price. For example, a representative of Dominica was a member of the International Whaling Commission. In exchange for a huge fisheries complex being built on his island by the Japanese, the Dominicans voted in favor of allowing a return to the taking of whales, much to the consternation of the U.S. members. Desperate needs drive desperate behavior.

A second conflicted issue involved deportees. Deportees are people who have come to the U.S., have entered illegally or committed a different crime, been arrested, tried, found guilty, and in some cases served jail time. When they are released from prison, if they are not U.S. citizens, they are deported, returned to their home country. *In most cases their countries do not want them back!* In fact, the governments tried to argue that these people came to the U.S. as youngsters, were corrupted in the U.S., turned to a life of crime in the U.S., spent time in our much more sophisticated criminal world, learned about criminal ways while in our prisons, and thus were a U.S. responsibility—forever. Research had been done on these individuals proving the argument to be without merit. The majority of those being returned home did not come to the U.S. until they were in their late teens or early twenties, they had already been in trouble with the law in their home country, and they had entered the U.S. In fact, their problems with local law enforcement often caused them to leave in the first place. When preparing for a deportee to return home, the U.S. was careful to inform local law enforcement and to provide the details of each individual situation before the person arrives in country. Countries created all kinds of barriers to prevent or indefinitely delay the return: no one available to meet them, no job is available to keep them busy, no family ties are left in country, etc. Those objections might all have been true, but we did not deport our own citizens, and under the circumstances, citizens of other countries appropriately were returned home. Intractable and confrontational situations: a genuine no win situation. As my Irish grandmother used to say, "When there is no solution, seek it lovingly."

A less confrontational, but instructive issue involved the import of beef, specifically bone-in beef, to Barbados. When the new Hilton Hotel opened, it had a world class restaurant that featured prime rib roast beef on the menu. It was an extremely popular item. After about two weeks, someone reported to the media that the restaurant was serving bone-in beef. *That prime rib actually had ribs!* And it was USDA prime beef. The government veterinarian immediately issued a public pronouncement that the import and the serving of the prime bone-in beef from the U.S. was against the law. The hotel was largely funded by the government, so there was no discussion. *Their roast no longer had ribs!*

Several other restaurants also served cuts of prime U.S. beef, including T-bone steaks. After this very public announcement, they were also prohibited from continuing. This prohibition somehow involved perceptions of the "mad cow" disease (which is only a problem in beef on the bone), and the import prohibition only applied to U.S. beef. Despite careful research by our economic staff, no history could be found of this prohibition. Was it a law? When was it passed? Who was responsible for its passage? We found no information, so had to assume it was a regulation promulgated by the veterinarian himself or someone in the Ministry of Agriculture. Meanwhile, imports of Canadian beef continued to be welcome in all forms.

The injustice of this really made me cross. I am an Iowan after all, and this situation was ludicrous. At the time there was only one case of mad cow identified in all of the U.S., and it was widely known that one cow came from a Canadian herd. What's up with that?

We set up a meeting with the Barbados government veterinarian, and I asked him to explain this to me. He had no explanation. When questioned, his first line of defense was "That's how it is." I refused to accept that as an explanation, so I pointed out the irony of the one cow with a problem coming from Canada. I asked him to do some research on the situation and he agreed. I was doubtful he would voluntarily get back to me so I marked my calendar to call him every other week. After several calls where we were told he was "out of the country" or tied up in meetings, I asked for a second meeting, at his convenience, but within the month. Apparently he decided there was no escaping me, so we met. Again, he could provide no reason for the prohibition, but was not willing to lift the ban. At my endlessly pleasant best, I suggested since the media was so interested in the prime rib being served at the Hilton, and at other restaurants, I was sure they would be equally interested in why all beef from Canada (with a much larger "mad cow" problem than the U.S.) was welcomed, while U.S. beef was not.

Most of the meat and grocery products came to Barbados from Canada, so we both understood that type of publicity would create no end of problems. He agreed to lift the ban, although I was unsuccessful in negotiating a timeline. Finally, through continuing pressure from me, along with several restaurant owners, U.S. bone-in beef is now welcomed in Barbados. A small victory, but one I enjoyed.

Next on my to-do list. Internet gambling. Antigua had licensed several American owned and managed casinos to operate in their country. The Antiguan government enjoyed the substantial revenue generated from these establishments and was very open when the management company proposed opening the American market to Internet gambling. The very rich U.S. market would enhance revenues both for the management company and for the government of Antigua exponentially. They rather naively expected the American market to be open to this initiative and were shocked and unhappy when it did not happen. The prime minister asked to meet with me and expressed his displeasure with the situation, warning me that his government was going to sue the U.S. government by taking their case to the World Trade Organization (WTO). After checking in with DOS, I responded that we appreciated their dilemma and they were certainly free to go to the court, but the U.S. had neither interest in nor intentions of legalizing Internet gambling.

I actually knew more about gambling that I needed or wanted to. Prior to my election to the Iowa Legislature, a lottery bill had been passed, making gambling legal in our state. The Iowa gaming law was narrowly constructed, referring only to the lottery. But according to federal law, if a state allowed any type of gambling, Native American Tribes in that state were free to begin any and all varieties of gaming on their lands. And in Iowa they did—in a big way. Then the horse breeders were convinced they could grow their industry if pari-mutuel betting was allowed. Gambling on the horses turned out not to be profitable, so, in the name of preserving the horse industry, they began a campaign to put slot machines at the race tracks. That passed. Then the representatives from Iowa's border districts wanted a share of the gambling revenues in the form of river boat gambling; so in a very few years, Iowa had more varieties of gambling than nearly any other state in the union. This expansion taught me many lessons, but the one most useful in Antigua was the fact that the states had jurisdiction over gambling regulation and they kept all the revenues so they weren't about to allow the federal government, or any foreign country, to intervene.

Antigua did go to the WTO and they won their case. The WTO said the U.S. was restraining trade by refusing to adopt Internet gaming. The decision was trumpeted far and wide. Tiny Antigua *defeated* the mighty U.S. Lots of "attaboys" and chest thumping going on in Antigua. After the decision, the Antiguans again expected the U.S. market would magically open to them. Not true. The states would not give up their prerogatives and the U.S. Congress was not about to take action to legalize Internet gambling. So Antigua determined that the U.S. stonewalled their opportunities and violated international trade agreements in the process.

Since the Antiguans persisted, and the Treasury Department in Washington represented the U.S. at the WTO, three lawyers from Treasury came to Antigua and asked me to meet them there. Over dinner one evening we discussed our strategy for the meeting with Antiguan government officials the next morning. Guess what? They expected me to conduct the meeting. They made it clear that nothing was going to change as a result of this meeting. I did not expect the Antiguans to cease their efforts, so what next?

The meeting was civil, and at the end of the three hours of discussion, we agreed to disagree. The Antiguan attorney general and I met with the media. We were both cordial, said it was a very productive meeting and discussions would continue. End of story. The issue evaporated.

Diplomatic efforts were so diverse, issues were sometimes so complex and intractable, that agreement was just not possible. In those cases, it was important to focus on the issues and not on the persons, or one could get very annoyed. Annoyance was rarely helpful. When we must agree to disagree, we do so knowing the difficult issues will continue to be difficult, but we can choose to work on things that can move forward to our mutual benefit.

CHAPTER TEN

MOTHER NATURE'S WRATH: IVAN HITS GRENADA

I had dealt with bureaucratic red tape, capricious heads of state, stubborn U.S. officials, unsafe working conditions, and inefficient systems. But nothing in my life's experience prepared me for the devastation that occurred when Hurricane Ivan destroyed Grenada. To make matters worse, I had just arrived back in Iowa for my annual medical check-up when Ivan landed. I repacked and got back on a plane. Hurricanes and other nasty weather caused all sorts of cancellations and delays, but after stops in Chicago, Washington-Dulles, Miami, Florida, Trinidad, and finally Barbados, I was back at work twenty-two hours after leaving Des Moines. I arrived in time to join my colleagues in the diplomatic corps in fly-over of Grenada to view the damage. We then landed and toured what we could on the ground, hoping to gather as much first hand knowledge as possible.

Grenada was actually considered outside the hurricane zone. It had been more than 50 years since a hurricane even approached the island. The government and the people were totally unprepared to survive the aftermath of such a storm.

What I saw was absolutely devastating. The lush forests and emerald green ground cover that had made the island so beautiful were destroyed. The hurricane stripped trees bare, and after the fallen leaves smothered ground vegetation, the sun cooked the detritus, leaving the region a hot, brown, steaming, stinking mess. Most buildings were completely demolished;

the ones remaining were missing roofs and windows. Many small homes had simply disappeared, along with everything in them. We learned that when roofs were lifted off buildings, the cyclone winds literally sucked out furniture and appliances, leaving behind empty buildings, only walls and floors remaining. The government had completed the annual distribution of school supplies and uniforms just three days before the hurricane; all of that was lost, and there was no money to replace it. But at the moment, the loss of school supplies seemed inconsequential since not one school building was habitable or safe. The same was true for medical facilities; hospitals and neighborhood clinics were destroyed. And strewn about everything were twisted, jagged chunks of metal, shards of glass and toppled telephone poles and power lines. Most homes in Grenada used corrugated metal for roofing. The pieces of the metal from those roofs became sharp, heavy, flying missiles in the high winds. Miraculously, there were few casualties. But many people were injured and most were in a state of shock, including the prime minster and other government officials. They, like everyone else, had seen their homes and possessions blown away. The government headquarters building lost a large portion of the roof, the windows were blown out, everything left inside was soaked by the rain and the building was without electricity, water, and telephone service.

The aftermath of Ivan was one of the most destructive things I've personally witnessed. The airport runway was cleared in about twelve hours, with a great deal of help from the U.S. Coast Guard. Consul General Fretz, along with the Regional Security Officers, traveled to Grenada and within 48 hours had organized and executed a process to evacuate over 1,000 Americans—in chartered planes from a badly damaged airport. It was a remarkable achievement by this group, many of whom slept on the floor at the embassy building. The evacuation was accomplished without electricity or telephones, working from a flooded airport terminal, with general panic in the streets, and in the absence of police or air traffic control officers. Those officials were at home in shock. There were no restaurants, food stores, or supermarkets, and the water supply was not potable. Yet the evacuation was accomplished.

In the following weeks and months, the resilience of the Grenadian people and the skills and compassion of our Office of Foreign Disaster Assistance (OFDA) and USAID teams were nothing short of heroic and miraculous. Every one of the U.S. Embassy employees in Grenada showed up for work the very next morning, and I later learned this was one of the only businesses where that happened. Many of the staff from Barbados went to Grenada immediately to help carry out the duties: The consul general, The RSO and his team, the OFDA and USAID staff and the MLO team who were working with the Coast Guards, ate meals ready to eat (MRE's) drank bottled water and slept in the embassy vehicles, or in chairs or on tables at the embassy (with a tarp for a roof) for many nights. These accomplishments, the personal sacrifices and devotion to duty that I witnessed from our people, made me proud to be American. I was deeply touched.

The U.S. stepped up to the plate, and in a big way. We made $250,000 in emergency funds available for use immediately. But that was only the beginning. Later, Congress would authorize millions in aid for Grenada and several other affected island countries. The airport runway was cleared and reopened only a day later, with help from the U.S. Coast Guard among many others. The first plane to arrive was filled with emergency supplies and USAID/OFDA workers. They were on the ground with supplies, food, water, and tarps to provide shelter from the sun and the rain. For several days the only available food was distributed from a warehouse building the U.S. Marines had built several years earlier. It had been built by U.S. Marines to withstand a Grade 4 hurricane and it did.

OFDA/USAID recovery workers were amazing people, and their methods are practical and down to earth. In particular, Julie Leonard, the OFDA officer stationed in Barbados, worked tirelessly and achieved miracles. After OFDA workers met, immediate emergency needs and had distributed as much emergency aid as possible, they began to plan for the ongoing recovery effort. They determined the size and scope of the problems and what had to be done in priority order. First and foremost, develop the logistics for the ongoing distribution of food and water that would be required for several months. It was not possible or efficient for Grenadians to continue to come to one location and wait in long lines. Aid needed to get to their neighborhoods. Next, identify which hotels or other buildings could reopen to house and feed workers coming in to provide assistance. La Source, what had been a lovely spa hotel, agreed they could provide this service. Part of the hotel had no roof, the spa area and swimming pool were filled with sand and debris, they were still without electricity, but by using a large generator, they provided rooms and breakfast and dinner buffets for whoever was on island to provide assistance. At times La Source looked like a mini United Nations, because assistance came from so many nations around the world.

On one occasion when I was staying overnight in Grenada, the host at LaSource was thrilled that he was finally able to provide me with an air conditioned room. I was thrilled too, because one doesn't sleep well in 90 degree nights. So, I dragged my suitcase up the hill, found my lovely, cool room, crawled into to bed and fell asleep almost instantly. The enjoyment lasted right up to the time I heard an unusual sound. I got up out of bed and put my feet in ice water. Somehow the air conditioner drainage system was clogged so the water was just flowing back into the room. I was *really* cool for a while, and my feet stayed cool for some time!

Meantime, USAID teams had arrived and were preparing to conduct classes to put people to work. First to be offered was construction skills training. We would teach people to rebuild their houses, schools and clinics. To their credit, Grenadians picked themselves up, lined up to participate in the training classes and learned to rebuild. They showed signs of renewed energy and hope. Their response and the results they produced were true miracles.

About a month after the hurricane hit, an international donor's conference was held in one of the government buildings that still had a roof. Temporary tent type walls were installed, a generator provided electricity that powered fans and air conditioning. Nearly 100 people gathered around tables set in a huge square. Spokespersons sat at the table with a staff person beside them, while more staff sat in chairs lining the walls. PM Mitchell presided. The purpose of the meeting was to determine what could be expected from each of the nations represented. I knew I was to be called on first because the U.S. Congress had already committed over $42 million to the nations that had been ravaged by Ivan. Since Grenada was by far the hardest hit, the lion's share of the money would come to them. It took me about eight minutes to speak my piece. And then I learned another lesson. The people who put the least money on the table are compelled to use the most air time explaining the magnificence of their gift. *Honestly!* Great Britain, Canada, and the European Union were all at the table. The United Kingdom was prepared to offer training, the Canadians were a little more generous, and the EU was prepared to provide quite a generous sum of money, but it would not be available for distribution for 12 to 18 months.

The U.S. was clearly going to be on point to make things happen. $42 million is a lot of money, a lot of support from U.S. taxpayers and a lot of money in support of a nation with less than 100,000 people.

Early in the recovery effort, Secretary Powell made a brief visit to Grenada to see the damage himself and have a firsthand view of how our money was being spent. His plane did a fly over of the island so he could see the devastation from the air. When he was flying over the island, he saw hundreds of blue tarps; they were everywhere. He told the folks working at the distribution center it was amazing to see all those blue tarps, each one saying the U.S. was providing shelter. They had accomplished miracles to get that many tarps out there in such a short time.

Near the distribution center, there was a tent city housing the combined forces of the Regional Security System. After his visit to the center, all the soldiers who were not on duty elsewhere on the island formed up to salute him. He walked over and thanked them for their work and then took the time to shake hands with every one of them. Secretary Powell, a son of Jamaican immigrants, was already well known and widely respected by most of those Caribbean men. They stood taller and saluted even more sharply as he left. At the end of the visit, he met with leaders of the government and some of the embassy staff at the airport. He thanked our staff for their fine work, both in preparing for his visit and for the work they were doing. They were thrilled to have their pictures taken with him. He then sat down with the government officials to discuss next steps. One of the ministers suggested they were in such trouble they should just return to growing bananas. Something they at least knew how to do. Secretary Powell sat up a little straighter, looked the man in the eye and said "Pull up your socks man. Look forward, be a leader, help these people grow something they can market." *I really admire this man!*

The rest of the story. I flew to Grenada at least once every week for 18 months following the hurricane. Each week I dropped by training classes funded and conducted by U.S. government trainers. There were classes offered for everything from taxi drivers learning tourist hospitality techniques, to people learning to stitch canvas making sails for sailboats of all sizes. There was training on how to repair fiberglass, since so many yachts and other vessels had been damaged. There was training for farmers; how to build shade houses so that flowers could be grown for export. The fields of anthuriums in many vibrant colors became a remarkable sight as training moved to action. I passed by construction sites to encourage workers and admire their work. I visited with people who were living in tents while rebuilding their homes. I went to school classes being held in tents, with children sitting on folding chairs and using clipboards or books for desks. A thorny legal issue arose regarding the rebuilding of homes. U.S. policy forbids the issuing of funds to rebuild houses if the persons who lived there had no clear title to the property. As it turned out, many Grenadians were in fact squatters, and had been for generations. So the legal titles had to be established before rebuilding could proceed. In the bigger picture with longer benefit, this effort clarified for many the issues of land ownership. Issues that had not been addressed perhaps for hundreds of years.

Since Kay was still home in Iowa, he organized drives at Rotary Clubs to collect much needed school supplies. He then arranged for shipments of the supplies to Barbados, where the local Rotary Clubs worked with the fishermen who volunteered their boats to deliver not only the school supplies but other needed goods as well.

I learned that disaster recovery experts insisted on reopening schools immediately, no matter what the conditions. A regular school schedule provided much needed structure for children and their families who must get organized enough to get their children to school and be sure they are properly clothed. This sense of normalcy also freed up parents to go to training classes or return to work. Regular school lunch programs provided the only meal of the day for many children during that time. These actions were the key to reestablishing hope. Somehow when we can go to school and church, we believe things will get better. Churches were also devastated, but no public moneys would be available to assist them. Still, all the congregations and parishes managed to find places to worship. And there were prayers of thanks for the fact that so many lives had been spared and the injured were healing. The embassy staff in Grenada was for the most part homeless, without even clothing for day to day needs. The embassy staff in Barbados stepped up and generously gave both goods and money in support of their colleagues in Grenada.

From my weekly visits and from the reports I received from the USAID teams onsite, I knew we were making great headway. But the prime minister asked to meet with me, and with great urgency. Of course I responded immediately, and since the topic was to be the reconstruction efforts, I took the USAID team leaders with me. He was in a meeting with several of his ministers, but interrupted the meeting when I arrived. The ministers joined our meeting as well.

He informed me the methods we were using to rebuild the country were destabilizing his government. We were providing funds without regard to *political loyalty.* I responded that was correct, we were using everyone who was willing and able to participate. He told me the situation had become so serious, he expected that henceforth, all reconstruction funds would be distributed through his government. It did not require great powers of deduction to figure out he wanted to distribute those funds to his supporters and not to members of the opposition.

I gave this a moment's thought and then I said, "You know, sir, the very last thing we want to do is destabilize your government. In fact, we don't even want to hear that word spoken." Pointing to my team leaders, I went on, "If we have caused problems for you, I can have these people and their teams out of Grenada within the week. Perhaps that might even be for the best, since that terrible tsunami in Asia left people in great need, and funds are badly needed there." I could see both my team leaders and his ministers turning pale and wringing their hands. And I thought to myself *"Can I really do that?"* My Irish temper was bubbling, making it hard to maintain that endlessly pleasant persona. But the prime minister interrupted me by saying loudly, "Oh Ambassador, you misunderstood my meaning. We are delighted with the progress and it must continue." His ministers nodded furiously and my teammates relaxed in their chairs. The meeting adjourned with much handshaking and friendly conversation. The destabilizing word was not heard again. My teammates were thrilled with me because they did not know how they would continue their work if the government held the money—and they would not receive any more criticism about how they were doing their jobs.

Eighteen months later, Grenadians were showing signs of getting back on their feet. Still much to do to return to pre-Ivan status, but teachers and children were back in their school buildings, the government headquarters building was functioning as before, the health clinics in the neighborhoods were reopened and were serving people regularly and something like 10,000 homes had been repaired or rebuilt. This was close to miraculous, and watching it unfold was a privilege, something I will never forget. The resiliency of the people, their smiles and waves as I drove by with the U.S. flag flying on the car, proud moments for me and for the U.S.

CHAPTER ELEVEN

THORNS IN MY SIDE

As a result of the process improvements we'd instituted, as well as some great work by colleagues, many of the issues I faced could now be dealt with in a matter of days or weeks. Others, however, dragged on for months, and despite my best efforts, some were still unresolved when I left.

One of those was the new embassy construction (NEC) project. The project predated me by several years, and progress was not discernable. This ineffectiveness was another highly visible example of how America's actions—or in this case, lack of them—was causing harm to our public reputation and our credibility with the people. Word on the street was that the local community was both amused and cynical about the status of the building. Most believed that the U.S. had no intention of ever completing it. About five years prior, one of my predecessors had asked for construction to stop while a lease-purchase agreement was finalized. The building we had leased was not completed, and construction had been stopped for nearly five years while we were paying rent of $500,000 per annum. Several years prior to my appointment, construction had begun anew. During my consultations in Washington I was assured the construction was underway and everything was in place to move full speed ahead.

Early in my stay, the Chief of Overseas Building Operations (OBO), who was in charge of new embassy construction around the world, came to inspect the progress. At his request we scheduled an all-employee meeting. He announced that we would move into the new building by January 2006. That was a huge disappointment. That meant *three more years* of construction, and worse, we would have to remain in the current decrepit facilities. We were promised that the construction pace would accelerate to meet that deadline.

After a few months passed with little progress, it became clear that even a January '06 move-in date wasn't going to happen. When I first arrived, I had raised the issues of unsafe work places and was told they would be short lived. There would soon be a new embassy. Three years hence did not meet my definition of soon! So I once again became the squeaky wheel. I began taking pictures of the unacceptable working conditions at the current embassy locations and emailing them to the head of OBO with emails telling him our people deserved better. As an employer we were putting our people at risk. I provided examples. The air conditioning units were covered with bird waste, with more added every day. I noted that three people had returned to the U.S. with serious respiratory illness. We were located in three separate buildings, each with major problems. The part of the embassy where my office was located was on the third and fourth floors of an abandoned bank building on the main street of Bridgetown (after the embassy was bombed in Nairobi and attacks occured on several other embassies, even those considered far from terrorism, certain rules and regulations had been put in place concerning the safety and security of embassy employees.) For Bridgetown, all the talk about street setbacks, fencing requirements, etc., were simply ignored. True, the embassy entrance was located a few feet down the street from the bank entrance. But often when I came to work in the morning, vagrants were sleeping on the steps of the bank entrance. The entrance to the annex where the administrative staff worked was located on an alley where trucks and cars often parked within five feet of the entrance and unloaded goods for the various businesses nearby. The consul general's office window was at the foot of an outdoor stairway on the building next door and the empty lot next to the building often had overgrowth as high as the windows.

Meantime, the people who lived around the construction site were voicing legitimate concerns about safety, traffic, the eyesore of the fencing surrounding the construction site and glaring lights that disturbed their sleep. After the government minister who represented the district called on me to share his constituents concerns, I decided to hold a town meeting with the neighbors. Once again, when I told the staff that I wanted to speak to the people directly, they were extremely uncomfortable with the idea. The security people were concerned someone might be angry enough to attack me, the public relations people were concerned how the media would cover it and the staff at the NEC was concerned they would be asked to do things they did not want to do. I was a little concerned about that last possibility myself. Still, the benefits outweighed the risks, so the town hall meeting was convened to listen to their concerns.

I asked the minister who had visited me to chair the meeting, to introduce the embassy staff in attendance and to set some ground rules. And he did, presiding over the entire meeting. There were some heated exchanges, but there were also legitimate concerns shared. In the end it was useful: I listened and learned. Some of the questions reflected rumors. For instance one woman asked, "Is it true there will be helicopters landing on the roof of the building regularly?" I responded "Good question. I love a question that allows a short answer. NO.!" People laughed and we moved on. Fortunately there were some very obvious and tangible things we could do to address the problems.

The concrete fencing would be painted so it wouldn't be such an eyesore. Embassy staff would mow the grounds outside the fence and plant some trees. The lights could be lowered and redirected to minimize the impact to neighbors. A parking lot could be completed rapidly to relieve some of the burden of workers parking on the street and clogging traffic.

After the meeting, Peter and I regularly drove through the neighborhood with diplomatic flags flying, so I could see that the things we had agreed to do were being done and the neighbors could see I was paying attention.

We painted the fence and regularly mowed and trimmed the area outside the fence. We even mowed a small open area which then would serve as a playground. We lowered and redirected the lighting so it was not shining directly into second story bedroom windows, and we used a media update to point out how much economic development was coming to the neighborhood in anticipation of our arrival. Two new restaurants and a health club had already opened. As I drove through the area people smiled and waved. When it came time for the actual move, there was no controversy and no negative publicity.

The enhanced security measures being undertaken for embassies around the world, that were being described to the Congress and the American public about embassies after the bombing in Nairobi, continued to be absent in Barbados. Months went by with no communication and with construction still moving at a snail's pace. I continued addressing my emails to OBO, *but I raised the volume on my squeaky wheel.* I began copying the State Department and the *White House.* My sense of urgency was not so much that it was taking an inordinate amount of time and money to get the thing built, although that should be of concern. My problem was the fact that our employees were working in unsafe and unsanitary conditions while we waited. Staff deserved safe and clean working conditions. The poor working conditions were never the fault of our administrative management team. They did an amazing job of maintaining what was there. Several years before, during the convoluted budget process, it had been determined there was a new embassy under construction, so maintenance and upkeep dollars were slashed.

I started visiting the site weekly, meeting with the general manager and asking for progress reports. At one point, they installed furniture and hung some of the artwork, so it would appear we were actually making progress. But I knew the sprinkler system had not been tested, the elevators didn't work and the back-up generators were in such a tight space that they overheated and shut down after operating for about thirty minutes. Just a few minor problems? Hmmm.

The squeaky wheel *finally* got oiled. New construction leadership arrived and I got credit for moving mountains. Maybe, but I was still watching for a noticeable change of pace. Fortunately, with the new leadership I got it. The site was cleaned up, workers moved with dispatch, the relationship with the local contractor was less cordial, but was more productive and businesslike, and I received regular reports on the problems and the progress. I began to have hope.

Still, the actual move didn't occur until months after my departure. No explanations were ever given and no one accepted accountability for a more than five year long, horrendously expensive construction process. Something was terribly wrong with this picture, and it still makes me angry when I think about it. People should not be asked to work under those conditions; with continual promises made that if they could just hang in there, the NEC would be completed shortly. For over five years. Not my definition of shortly. The whole process lacked openness and integrity.

The NEC today is a lovely and useful building outfitted with the latest technology and decorated with art from local painters and sculptors. People finally have a safe, functional workplace. Kay and I have since visited the new building and it is a practical and functional workplace.

Another big thorn in my side was the C-26 program. C-26 is the label for a certain type of airplane. The C-26 model had been replaced in many locations by the U.S. military, and with the help of the Narcotics Affairs Section (NAS), several of the planes had been relocated to the Caribbean so the Regional Security Services (RSS) could use them to participate with U.S. and other partners to conduct nighttime fly overs observing illicit drug trafficking by sea. The U.S. and the United Kingdom military provided training, and RSS members became expert pilots and learned to handle their own simple maintenance tasks. The trafficking of drugs, money and people are all part of a logistical chain that is almost as sophisticated as Wal-Mart's. There are the growers, the handlers, the transportation people, the finance people, the wholesalers and the retailers. The C-26 pilots regularly flew night missions to interrupt the transportation arm of this deadly chain. The C-26 crews worked hand in hand with Caribbean law enforcement officers, the U.S. Drug Enforcement Agency, and drug enforcement personnel and the Coast Guards from the Netherlands, the United Kingdom, France, and Belgium. The patrols were designed to stop, or at least slow, drug traffic from Central and South America to the U.S. and Europe. Much of the trafficking through the Eastern Caribbean went to the retail dealers in Great Britain, so the Brits were very interested in the program and sought to provide support for it.

The C-26 program had achieved several very successful missions, where they identified the traffickers, the nearest ship zeroed in and arrests were made. These successes were regularly featured in the local media. A group of Marines built permanent hangars for Barbados's two planes. I wrote earlier about welcoming the Marines to Barbados. At long last the door for the hangars had arrived and been installed. Now it was time to move the planes to the new hangars. The RSS leadership scheduled a ribbon-cutting ceremony that included much pomp and circumstance, had many government officials and all the local media in attendance to celebrate the occasion. And then, irony of ironies, the very next day I was informed that the money for the program had disappeared from any budget—not even the named line item remained. I was told I needed to inform the local authorities of this change. Talk about a difficult message to deliver. The U.S. government had instituted and funded the program, the U.S. Marines had built the hangar and turned it over to the locals, and we were pulling the plug. In fact, I was told the RSS should consider themselves lucky if they got to keep the airplanes.

Even more egregious, it soon became obvious why the money disappeared. NAS bureaucrats had earmarked the C-26 funds for friends who wanted a consulting contract. The friends who got the job and the money were the only winners in this situation. A functioning and effective program was lost, and diplomatic relations between the U.S. and the small nations of the Eastern Caribbean were irrevocably harmed. It appeared, correctly, that our right hand did not know (or care) what our left hand was doing.

Unfortunately, this kind of sleight-of-hand is hardly uncommon. Many people who worked in the DOS and other agencies were outstanding public servants that have given years of loyal and steadfast service. I admire and respect them. They listen to people in the field and respond as they can. But there are others who knowingly manipulate the budgeting systems to meet their own (and their friends') best interests. They accomplish this simply by outlasting leadership; knowing they can count on windows of opportunity occurring when the new and uninformed leadership is appointed and getting oriented. In spite of my frustration and my best efforts, there was little I could do to fix the C-26 problem. The bureaucrats simply hunkered down and kept doing what they've always done: ignoring the best interests of the Foreign Service, their agency, and their country.

CHAPTER TWELVE

"SEE YOU LATER MON" – RETURNING HOME

In late May of 2006, I received a call from White House Personnel asking me if I had plans and intentions for my length of service. Kay and I had talked about this and determined we would be ready to return home at the end of my three-year term, December 2006. We loved Barbados and the people we'd met, but we felt we'd accomplished much, and year end would be our time to return home, to rejoin family and friends. Since I knew from experience that a lengthy amount of time was necessary for a new appointee to move through the confirmation process, I told them I hoped we could do some succession planning. Perhaps we could plan the succession so there would not be a long time between my departure and my successor's arrival. I was assured that would be entirely appropriate and I was thanked profusely for my service and told repeatedly I was doing a great job.

Later that summer when I was in D.C. for an ambassador's conference, I met with a potential appointee for my position. We had a nice conversation over lunch about the job and agreed that if her confirmation went smoothly, she would arrive in Barbados after the Christmas holidays. I continued to communicate with her through email, keeping her updated on issues and events, and planning for an orderly handover of responsibilities. But little in Washington goes as planned. Her confirmation occurred in mid-October, and the next day she indicated she expected me to be gone in two weeks. I reminded her of our agreements and our email correspondence, and explained that I had made several very public commitments—among them a pending Article 98 signing and two piano performances for major fundraisers for island charities. I didn't mention that our family had planned to be with us for the holidays and for my farewell tour. But it was all for naught: she was insistent on an earlier departure.

I felt I was being summarily dismissed by my successor. The White House had much bigger and more important issues to resolve than arbitrating the transition of a Caribbean ambassador, so I acquiesced and agreed to a very quick exit. My exit was far from the gracious leave-taking I had envisioned. I did visit each island, sometimes visiting several islands in a single day; if only for a very brief handshake with government officials. With the very short notice I could provide, some of the people I needed to thank were traveling and not available. Still, there was the welcome sense of having accomplished much and of leaving behind greatly improved relationships with governments and individuals.

In Barbados, after it became known I was leaving so abruptly, we were treated to multiple daily farewell events. Kay and I enjoyed lunches and dinners, received engraved plates and plaques, certificates and personal notes of appreciation. Every day, Bajans, expats who live and work in Barbados, public officials and private citizens, often people we'd never met, stopped us on the street or on our way in and out of meetings to let us know how much our service was valued and what a difference we'd made. It was touching and much appreciated. Several of our family members dropped everything and made the trip to Barbados to join us for our farewell reception at the residence, a celebration that included the annual Marine Birthday event. Frankly, I was deeply hurt by the whole situation and terribly disappointed not to be able to complete my engagements, or enjoy the final visits of family and friends. Still, I left with a great feeling of achievement, knowing we made a positive difference.

We returned to Washington for several final consultations, the debriefing phase. And we were treated to a lovely and gracious retirement ceremony at DOS. Kay was presented a magnificent U.S. flag and I was presented with my very own Chief of Mission flag. Both flags stand proudly in our home today, beside the steel pan drum.

To complete the circle, when we left Washington, we returned to Hilton Head Island for a week of rest and relaxation, back to where that first fateful telephone call came from the White House. Only now we had wonderful memories, a new appreciation for a fabulous life experience, and a sense of accomplishment. There is really nothing we could do or say that could come close to sharing our appreciation for the opportunity to serve.

And so we returned to Iowa, back home to family and friends. Slipping back into the routines, I realized there are some things, beyond friends and family, that I had really missed. First and foremost, being able to go into the garage, get in my car and drive myself wherever I want to go. No appointment, no one checking on arrival and departure times. No nagging thoughts about our safety and security. And no matter how much I appreciated Peter (and I truly appreciated him), I do love having the independence of driving myself. We also missed the opportunity of being alone and in our own home again.

I actually enjoy menu planning, grocery shopping and cooking in my own kitchen again. Things that often seemed like a nuisance before, now are enjoyable: entertaining friends and family at our own dining room table is fun.

One final process story. Throughout my posting, my salary was paid through electronic funds transfer (EFT) to our bank in West Des Moines. Kay had served on the board of our bank prior to our leaving, and we received terrific and personal attention through all the intricacies of international banking. When we finally arrived home, and Kay was reviewing our bank statements, he realized I was still being paid. Four weeks after my retirement ceremony, the regular bi-weekly EFT was still taking place. We waited for another two weeks to make sure we had the correct timing of pay periods and my resignation date. Then I called DOS to report I was still being paid. I was thanked for my call and assured the matter would be taken care of. Then another deposit was made. We joked that perhaps they were going to pay us until the end of the year, even though my successor insisted on arriving early. That would work, right? Yes, we were joking! And then another payment was made. Long story shorter, I continued to receive salary via EFT until the middle of April of the following year. Two huge folders of correspondence and email documenting my efforts to get it stopped notwithstanding, it did not stop. During this time, of course, Social Security, income tax deductions (both state and federal) health insurance payments, and pension contributions continued to occur. After consulting with our attorney, we decided there was no choice but to file our federal and state income tax returns timely, even though we knew we would no doubt be expected to pay all that money back at some point and had no notion how the IRS would view this fiasco. Finally, I asked our lawyer to join me on a telephone conference call and demanded to speak directly to the payroll supervisor. Once again I described the problem. Two weeks later the email came indicating the EFTs had been stopped. A fax soon followed outlining the amount I would be expected to pay back. Adding insult to injury, I was told I had two weeks to return the money before interest would begin accruing. *As if I had created the problem!* Then, taxes and Social Security taxes became an issue. Did we have to file amended tax returns? Pay all the fees again, in order to have the mistake corrected? By this time, I was irate. If there were to be any fees paid, legal fees for resolving IRS or social security difficulties, I expected DOS to take care of them. At the end of the day I was issued a letter that indicated the error was on the part of the government, and I should not be held responsible or required to amend or adjust either my tax returns or adjust the Social Security deductions. We were told that if there were repercussions at a later time, the letter should suffice. I wondered aloud if the DOS and the IRS were on speaking terms and hoped I would not have to find out. A second tax reporting year has now passed with no further issues, but I have kept all the correspondence, the letter from DOS to me and to my attorney, and we will have our fingers crossed for the next five years, hoping we are out of the woods!

CHAPTER THIRTEEN

I TRY NOT TO GET OUTRAGED MORE THAN ONCE A MONTH

I learned a great deal during my three years as a United States ambassador. It was a continual and steep learning curve. But as it happened, the values and the skills that served me well during my tenure were values and skills I have believed in and practiced throughout my life. I reconfirmed my belief in the leadership practices that had served me well in other positions. I also reconfirmed my opinions of leadership practices that do not work. Leadership skills that are effective are the same worldwide.

The education I received throughout my tenure as ambassador came fast and furious, and left no part of my life untouched, personally or professionally. It was invaluable and humbling. As a final chapter in my experience, I want to share at least a few of the lessons and values that were most important in helping me get the job done.

It's important to accept and appreciate the advantages of a job that confers the benefits of royalty, but not be seduced by them.

People stood when we entered the room. Our house staff was anxious to please and worked hard to anticipate our needs, to provide constant service. The driver who also served as a bodyguard would graciously appear at any hour of the day or night to drive me wherever I needed to go. It would have been easy and comfortable to assume I had personally done something to earn such treatment—or that it was all about me, or even worse, I somehow "deserved" all that attention. In fact, it was all about respect for the position. I was the personal representative of the president of the greatest nation on earth. Such royal treatment could easily change a person (as it often does), allowing you to believe that whatever you want to do is acceptable (as many have done). One could attend the cocktail parties, enjoy the lovely dinners, stay at the fabulous resorts, preside at outstanding events, host memorable social occasions, cut the ribbons, and decide that's all that was needed. For me, and I believe for most ambassadors, both political and professional, it was a unique opportunity to serve my country. The pressure I felt not only to get the job done, but to excel, was greater than at any other job I'd held. As I have said, the buck absolutely stopped with me. Issues of critical importance to America and the Caribbean fell to me and if I didn't accomplish the mission it was not going to be accomplished. This was heady stuff for the ex-schoolteacher from Iowa. I felt personally responsible for the interruption of money-laundering and of drug trafficking, for identifying and communicating terrorist activity in the region, for repairing and improving America's image abroad, for bolstering the Caribbean economy and improving the lives of its people. No small task. But, with the help of many—the really remarkable members of a fabulous country team, a loyal embassy staff, both Americans and Bajans, the Marines and the staff at the residence—we made remarkable progress.

It's important to take a stand, to work to change things for the better. And when something is not right - to work at solving problems.

When it comes to the behemoth in Washington, with all its power and its deeply entrenched methods, it would have been much easier to blend in with the masses and just go along for the ride. There are powerful incentives to do so: job security and promotions are the rewards for those who maintain the status quo. But what I experienced convinced me that the way Washington does business is a serious hindrance to creating positive change in the field. Perhaps a hindrance to continuing our way of life. After I became an insider and began to understand how the bureaucracy works, I felt obligated to shine the light on the things that hindered progress and hurt employees, and to try to do something about them. The simplest course of action (and the one that would have been smiled upon) would have been to do nothing, but my long held bias for action just would not allow me to sit by while we were not performing our jobs efficiently and effectively, we could not achieve the goals we set for ourselves and the best interests of employees weren't being considered. There's a time and place for "Iowa nice," and as a rule I rely on diplomatic methods to seek and achieve solutions. *Except when I don't!* Yes, there's a time and place for Iowa nice—and actually, it's most of the time—but there's also a time and place to take a stand and to do so clearly and firmly. I kept my cool most of the time, *except when I didn't.* Both methods were effective for me, as long as the latter was used only sparingly.

It's important to know that despite the rampant anti-Americanism that we hear and read about all over the world, America is still viewed as <u>the</u> land of opportunity.

"Yankee go home" might still be a catch phrase, but for us it was always followed by *"and when you go, take me with you."* When I was on island, the furor over the Iraq War was perhaps at its height. People were making speeches in the parliaments opposing our presence there, and the letters to the editor in the local paper were negative and sometimes downright nasty. The radio call-in shows were a series of shouting matches: few of them in support of the U.S. position. Many people of the Caribbean nations were deeply opposed to the war, (that regime change fear again) and America's image had taken a beating. Despite all this, most of the people of the Caribbean viewed America (which most of them thought only included Miami, Washington, D.C., New York City, and *maybe* the Carolinas) as an almost magical land where everything good was still possible. The question was asked more than once, "You're from Iowa. Is that in the United States?" America is considered *the* place to go; for work, for education, for joining family members who have been fortunate enough to precede them—or even to do some Christmas shopping. The appetite for visas is huge. Even though I had been warned about this, I had no idea how many requests and panic-stricken stories I'd hear, or how many influential persons wanted special treatment or would seek my assistance for a friend, a grandchild, someone who required medical treatment, etc. It was truly humbling to realize how many people outside our country are absolutely convinced that opportunities abound in the U.S. *I agree with them.* We are very much the land of opportunity, we do believe our rights come from our Creator and not from our government. And one of them is the God-Given right to the pursuit of happiness. Sometimes I fear the belief in the opportunities of America is larger and deeper among people abroad than it is in the U.S. And sadly, sometimes it seems there are Americans who see their country as the land of entitlement, not the land of opportunity.

It is important to build relationships with members of the host governments. It is equally and perhaps more important to build relationships and friendships with grass roots citizens, to become engaged in the society. Both sets of relationships are needed to accomplish our diplomatic mission.

In my first campaign for the Iowa State Senate, I walked the neighborhoods of my district and visited with people at their front doors for 100 nights in a row. I would start at 4:30 in the afternoon and stay out until the street lights came on. By the time the campaign was over, I had knocked on every door in my district. This is just the way we campaign in Iowa, and if it weren't, I'd probably do it anyway. There's no better way to connect with the people than, well, to connect with the people. The Internet and Facebook are great, but nothing replaces face time. In the Caribbean, Kay and I attended nearly everything we were invited to, if we could fit it into our schedule. We found and enjoyed volunteer opportunities; we sometimes did our own grocery shopping. Time and again, people expressed surprise at our emphasis on collegiality and communication. I actually *enjoy* working a room: a fact of life that Kay sometimes considers a character flaw.

> *The best and most important programs and funding the embassy provides are those things that help the Caribbean people help themselves so they can independently continue to apply the learning and use the tools.*

After the Berlin Wall fell, the U.S. was for a time the only world superpower. As such, expectations around the world were huge—assistance for everything, for economic development, support for law enforcement, education programs, the list goes on and on. This was especially true among these small island nations. At first it seemed that I listened to a letter to Santa Claus at every visit I made to government officials. Could you build us a police station? Pave our roads? Improve our airport? Build us a school? Train and equip a Coast Guard? Build a Cricket Oval? Just send us the money. All good ideas and no doubt useful to their countries. There never seemed to be enough program funds to do all these things. *Nor should there be.* I often asked myself which of these things had a high enough priority, which ones served the highest purpose or which ones had the highest likelihood of sustainability. And as I considered all the options, which ones justified providing U.S. tax dollars?

I struggled with the idea that economies of scale suggested these small Caribbean countries were not large enough to internally support the infrastructure necessary for truly independent nations. For instance, respect for the rule of law requires competent law enforcement, public health requires clean water and health care providers, clinics and hospitals, economic development requires an infrastructure of roads and utilities, dependable electricity requires infrastructure and skilled workers, and democracy requires educated citizens to participate. Often, these necessities weren't in place, which put a country's leader in the position of Chief Executive Fundraiser, travelling the world asking for money. And they spent a lot of time and money doing it. It amazes me how many organizations exist in the world whose mission it is to provide financial assistance to emerging democracies. I'm all for fiscally supporting a country in a time of need, but I'm convinced that in the long run, the best course of action supports people in finding jobs so they can stimulate their own economies and help themselves. Helping them become self-sustaining, willing and able to invest in their own country is a wonderful gift that keeps on giving. Certainly one that lasts beyond any one individual's term of office.

I learned that many of the skills I relied on to be an effective ambassador were things I'd learned as a child in the arms of America's heartland.

Who would ever have predicted that Mary Kramer from small-town Iowa would make it to the top tiers of business and politics? Surely not me. By the time all was said and done, I realized that my life's experiences couldn't have happened in any other place or in any other way. Only in America does one get to know personally the man who will become President of the United States. And after working with him briefly, have him remember who I am and choosing to appoint me to represent him. Humbling, to say the least.

I was brought up with strong religious beliefs and convictions, yet I was also taught to be respectful and appreciative; and while many people advocate an aggressive, confrontational, no-holds-barred attitude in business and in politics, for me "Iowa nice" has been infinitely more effective.

Civil conversations and mutual respect are absolutely crucial for diplomacy, for business, and for the simple interactions of everyday life. If I had come out swinging (and I was sorely tempted) in some of my encounters with the business and government leaders of the Caribbean, I know my opportunities to be effective would have been instantly and irreparably damaged.

Three years as an ambassador also reinforced my belief that civil discourse is necessary to good government and to healthy societies. Little that is good or sustainable happens without respectful disagreement and discussion; without communication skills that include being willing and able to listen. My personal commitment to civil discourse served me well over many years in employee negotiations, in solving disciplinary problems, in coaching for improved performance, in resolving many a contentious session in the Iowa Senate, and in raising my children. That commitment influenced much of the work during my service as U.S. ambassador.

I believe:

• open and respectful communication is the foundation for productive and lasting change;

• *listening* is the **most** important leadership and diplomatic skill; and

• addressing serious and confrontational issues with urgency—without excuses or placing blame—earns the respect of all involved.

These are the things that served me well and allowed me to serve others well.

So, dear readers, in the future, when you engage in discussions with elected officials or candidates for office, and I surely hope you do, question them about their willingness and desire to change the intractability of the current processes and systems in Washington, at your state capital, and in your local governments. Without your voice, the voice of the constituent, the processes and systems and the people who operate within them will simply continue as they are, waiting for the next election or the next appointee. Bureaucracy continues operating as it always has until something, or someone, comes along to intervene.

If you take away only one thing...

It is this. Every time we elect a new administration, Democrat or Republican, the president has the opportunity, the responsibility for filling just over 8,000 positions through the appointment process. 8,000 is a very *large number.* No matter what the party, many of those people will be appointed as reward for political loyalty and hard work, as much as for their experience and skills, and the huge majority of political appointees consider themselves to be "policy" people. They serve at the pleasure of the president and above all, they want to represent his positions, perhaps even influence his policy positions. It is rare when they have an interest in the mundane work of management, of providing leadership that seeks to make changes that will lead to a culture of productivity, of having the persistence to insist on the tedious process changes that require constant monitoring, or in becoming the champion of *outstanding* employees.

Why should *you* care or even be interested in these arcane process questions? I'll tell you. In government today, nothing, no department, no project, ever goes away. Instead, the people and the structures of the old stay in place, and when something new is required, a *new* group of employees is appointed or hired to do the next "new thing"; whatever that next new thing might be. A slightly updated version of an old nursery rhyme seems fitting, and brings a smile.

"Mary, Mary, Quite Contrary.
See How the Bureaucracy Grows?"

Without purposeful and intentional change in the appointment processes, a change that includes appointing people who are expected to take responsibility for change, the bureaucracies will continue to grow. People talk about smaller government and lower taxes. Both of those things are possible, but they will be temporary and lead only to pyrrhic victories unless we find courageous leaders that understand and accept the complexity of the problems, and are willing and able to tackle them.

CHAPTER FOURTEEN

THANK YOU AMERICA

I am extremely proud of the people who represent America overseas. They are dedicated and hardworking. They know their jobs and they earn the respect of their peers in Embassies and their colleagues in host governments every day. I was blessed with two outstanding Deputy Chiefs of Mission, Marcia Bernicat and Meg Gilroy, and two efficient and effective office management specialists, Bonita Estes and Nancy Doe. All four of these women enhanced my ability to accomplish important tasks and increased my efficiency immeasurably. Their guidance and support was invaluable, and all four have blessed me by becoming my lifelong friends.

The Marines that serve in embassies around the world, certainly in Bridgetown, are an elite group of young men and women who are carefully selected and well trained for their task, protecting U.S. Embassies and information vital to national security around the world. Their service, in every embassy and in every theater of operation around the world is exceptional, and I thank them.

U.S. foreign policy, done well, has a heart. That strategy is much more than trade or economic and trade policies. International trade and financing are important and necessary. But our higher calling is working together with our neighbors to make things better among the poorest in the world. When we do that well, things will be better and *safer* for all of us. So, we promote democratic ideals that allow individual citizens to decide for themselves what is best for them. We promote free enterprise as the perpetual engine for economic growth. We help others to develop a constructive and positive vision of the desired future. I believe this is the formula for achieving freedom and peace in the world.

Young people around the world, who see themselves as entrepreneurs and who have hope for their future, cannot be recruited in their countries or on the Internet as terrorists or suicide bombers.

Is this hard work? Does it demand patience? Is our will to stay the course tested often? Yes.

The culture and values we share and enjoy in America are never seen or read about in the international media. Through cable television, and the Internet, people in foreign countries see U.S. news, pretty much all bad from New York, Washington, Los Angeles and Miami, and believe that represents all of America. Parents killing their children, home invasions, shootings on the streets, Lindsay and Brittany, rock stars, and the culture of Hollywood are all seen and accepted as an accurate portrayal of American culture throughout the world. Because there is virtually no offsetting information in the public media, it becomes even more important we invest in winning "hearts and minds." In this investment, our government is not the only institution that can make a difference. In fact it's not even the best way to make that difference. Individual citizens, churches, associations and advocacy groups all contribute to winning hearts and minds. Travelling abroad, participating in mission trips, providing aid and assistance through volunteer organizations, making friends and building one on one relationships—these are best, most effective methods of winning the hearts and minds of others. By sharing our own.

Why does this matter?

Before we experienced living overseas, and we were blessed to live very well, I took for granted the things my parents taught me, things that were enhanced during the years I was receiving a marvelous public education.

My appreciation of the blessings of liberty, of being American, has grown exponentially with this experience. I am ashamed of the complacency, the self satisfaction I took with me. I simply accepted all I had, the blessings of opportunity and of liberty, forgetting or ignoring how it was earned, who earned it, and who continues the work of earning it today.

At the end of the experience, I am more deeply committed to my country than ever before in my life.

It was thrilling to be able to offer the small countries I worked with a positive vision of freedom, of the right to define your own future and the tools to build it. That was as it should be. It was an investment that will bear returns into the foreseeable future. America is a revolutionary country—conceived by our founders to advance the cause of individual liberty. In the words of Thomas Jefferson, "I have sworn upon the altar of God eternal hostility against every form of tyranny over the mind of men."

Nothing brought that home to me more forcefully than being privileged to have our young Marines present our flag before me. It brought tears to my eyes every single time. Their respect for their country and their tasks was reflected in the precision and pride they took in performing them. As I looked into those young faces, I knew they had volunteered their lives to protect mine —and yours.

Serving as a U.S. ambassador is a privilege few are able to share, a truly remarkable life experience. Our lives were changed in many ways. Perhaps most significant; our increased sense of obligation to continue to seek justice and liberty.

Teddy Roosevelt said "Far and away the best prize life can offer is the chance to work hard at work worth doing." Diplomacy is work worth doing, for when it fails, the consequences are many—even the armed conflicts we call war.

As Americans, we owe an extraordinary debt to those generations who brought us to the edge of this new and Promised Land. Their sacrifices not only brought us a good life, but through war and hard times, they kept our values alive. Those values are the greatest gift we can pass on.

It is our task to preserve them and to pass them on to future generations. In America, and throughout the world.